Strikemakers & Strikebreakers

SIDNEY LENS

illustrated with photographs

Lodestar Books   E. P. Dutton   New York

LIBRARY OF CONGRESS CATALOGING IN PUBLICATION DATA

Lens, Sidney.
   Strikemakers & strikebreakers.

   "Lodestar books."
   Bibliography: p.
   Includes index.
   Summary: Describes the origins and history of strikes in the United States and discusses their purpose, effectiveness, and how their resolutions affect the relationship between employees and their employers.
      1. Strikes and lockouts—United States—Juvenile literature.   2. Strikebreakers—United States—Juvenile literature.   [1. Strikes and lockouts.   2. Strikebreakers]
I. Title.   II. Title: Strikemakers and strikebreakers.
HD5324.L39   1985   331.89′2973   84-28618
ᵀSBN 0-525-67165-X

Published in the United States by E. P. Dutton,
a division of NAL Penguin Inc.,
2 Park Avenue, New York, N.Y. I0016

Published simultaneously in Canada by
Fitzhenry & Whiteside Limited, Toronto

Editor: Virginia Buckley   Designer: Riki Levinson

Printed in the U.S.A.   COBE   First Edition
10 9 8 7 6 5 4 3 2

✓   34697000024599

to A. J. Muste
and my little immigrant mother,
who fought the sweatshops

Contents

1 The Origin of Strikes

Men strike in order to escape from a situation they feel
to be intolerable. . . . Contented men do not strike.
George W. Taylor, *Are Workers Human?*

Consider this tale of two strikes:

In 1956 the United Steelworkers of America called a national
steel strike. Among those on the picket line were workers of four
companies—Bethlehem, Youngstown Sheet and Tube, Inland,
and Republic—who had fiercely resisted the advance of the steel
union nineteen years earlier. Many of the strikers vividly remem-
bered the Little Steel strike of 1937, when seventy thousand workers "hit the bricks" because the companies refused to recognize
their union.

That earlier strike had been a bloody affair. The National
Guard was called out to challenge the strikers in many places,
including six cities in Ohio alone. Employers organized vigilante
groups to break picket lines, and violence flared in scores of steel
towns. Two hundred strikers were arrested in Youngstown alone.

During the 1937 Little Steel strike, 10 strikers were killed by police and many were wounded on Memorial Day near the Republic plant in South Chicago.   UNITED STEELWORKERS OF AMERICA

On Memorial Day that year, a line of pickets was halted near the Republic plant in South Chicago, and before the shooting had stopped, police killed 10 workers and wounded 160 more. The strikers and their friends had been shot in the back while running away from tear gas. Elsewhere 8 other strikers were killed. The strike was defeated.

Now in 1956, Republic urged its blue-collar employees—all covered by union contracts by this time—to take their vacations during the strike so that they wouldn't lose any pay. There seemed to be little animosity between labor and management, despite the work stoppage. At the South Works mill of U.S. Steel in Chicago, the company furnished the picket captain with a desk just inside the gate, and ran a power line and water to the union's six trailers. One night it supplied the pickets with beer. In another mill, management provided portable toilets for the men and women who walked off the job.

Attitudes and opinions obviously change, especially on such controversial issues as strikes. At one time, employers may fight unions hammer and tongs; at another they may seek conciliation, as in the 1956 steel strike. There are no fixed attitudes—on the part of management, labor, or the public.

At one time, the courts declared that strikes were illegal conspiracies. Today they are considered legal, but there are still questions that many people ask about them.

For instance, Should police and firemen be allowed to strike? If they are, who will protect people in the streets against pickpockets and murderers? Who will put out the fires? Some unionists say the government could use the National Guard or state police to keep order during a police strike. There have been a few occasions during strikes of firemen when police or the National Guard were called on to douse fires.

But the public generally is opposed to strikes by police and fire fighters, and usually unions who represent them agree to give up the right to strike in favor of arbitration. Instead of a work stoppage, the issue is put before an impartial arbitrator who hears the arguments on both sides, then issues a binding decision.

But if there is general agreement that police and fire fighters should not strike, what about strikes of teachers or of other government workers? There are more than 15 million of them—about 1 of 7 workers in the country. Many states and the federal government have laws prohibiting strikes by government employees. Nonetheless they do take place, and the public is often sympathetic to teachers, for instance, who feel that they have no other recourse. It would be inconsistent to declare strikes of public-school teachers illegal, but strikes of private- or parochial-school teachers legal. Should teachers and public workers, then, be allowed to strike? Should they be forced to accept arbitration? How do you decide such an issue?

There are also some questions of strategy to consider. For instance, Should unions give up the strike weapon in favor of collaboration with employers—as many unions do in Japan? Would workers have more security and higher pay if they operated in harmony with their employers, rather than at arm's length? American unions do not consider the Japanese example a good one. They say that workers in Japan do not really have jobs for their lifetime as claimed, especially in the smaller shops, and that they are forced to work at an exceptionally fast pace.

Another question often asked is, Does the strike weapon still suit the needs of modern America? What happens when workers strike a company or an industry—like steel—that is dying, that is no longer competitive with similar companies in Japan or Germany or France? If the unions insist on higher wages in such circumstances, won't they be driving their employers out of business? In fact, since 1979 many unions have taken wage cuts or given other concessions to keep their companies in normal operation. No one knows just where this trend will end, but many in the labor movement believe it has gone far enough. They are opposed to further concessions. If an employer wants to stay in business, they say, let him modernize his plant to keep up with competition. Some unions, like the machinists' union, have unveiled plans to modernize the entire American economy.

There is also the question of whether strikes are outdated for other reasons. Originally a single union matched its economic power against a single company or industry—let's say the carpenters' union in Chicago against the construction industry in Chicago. But corporations have become immense. Some operate enterprises in many industries or many countries. A strike against only one of their enterprises in one country or city hardly hurts them. In addition the situation is complicated by the fact that computers and robots are doing away with some jobs entirely. Under these circumstances, some unionists say that labor should shift its emphasis from strikes to politics—should form a political party of its own, a Labor party, to defend jobs, wages, and social benefits.

There are no easy answers.

Ordinarily there are one thousand to six thousand strikes a year in the United States, involving 1 to 6 million workers. Considering that the labor force has varied from 50 million to 110 million, the number of strikers constitutes anywhere from 1 or 2 percent of employed workers to as much as 8 percent.

That may not be a large figure. Still every strike is an inconvenience to someone. When bus drivers strike, passengers have to drive to work in their own cars, hitch a ride, or stay home. When railroad workers strike, perishable foodstuffs rot in freight cars, and consumers not only face shortages but pay more for fruits and vegetables. The workers on strike, of course, don't get paid during walkouts, and their bosses suffer a cut in business and profits.

Why then do workers strike?

Why do employers try to break strikes?

Workers do not leave their jobs and walk picket lines without a good reason. Strikers have wives or husbands to support, children to feed, mortgages to pay, installment payments to meet; they don't give up weekly paychecks for a lark. They have to have very serious reasons for doing it.

It is naive to say that workers strike because union leaders tell them to strike. The normal practice of most unions is to strike only if the members vote to strike. A small number of strikes are called by labor leaders on their own. But contrary to the general impression, most union officials try to avoid strikes—if only because a strike means more work for them, more trouble.

It is also wrong to assume that employers try to break strikes because they want to defend their workers from union bosses or to guarantee workers the right of free choice. It is much more simple that that. They break strikes in order to earn more money; every dollar that goes for raises means that much less in profits. And they break strikes in order to retain control of their operations. They don't want unions telling them that they cannot fire an older worker if they can hire a younger one more cheaply. They don't want to discuss safety issues with a union or take up grievances with union leaders. In sum, it's not a matter of high principle, but of dollars and cents—and control.

Over the years, tens of thousands of people have been killed, injured, or arrested, and millions of dollars in property have been destroyed or damaged in strikes. That's a high price for society to pay. Why, then, does the government permit strikes? Why doesn't it outlaw them and require employers and unions to submit their disputes to a government agency or an arbitrator for a binding decision?

That's a good question. The first problem is how to determine what is a fair wage. Is it what the worker needs to support his family adequately or what the boss needs to earn a fair profit? And what is a "fair" profit? It's all very complicated. In our society we have been satisfied to have wages determined by the market—by supply and demand—just as the price of a pair of shoes or a hat is determined.

The second problem has to do with freedom. Can we have a free society if the government controls the lives of employers and employees—the two most important forces in our economy? Not likely. It is significant that no strikes and no unions were permitted in Nazi Germany under Hitler, or in Fascist Italy under Mussolini. The only way to effect a change was to organize a revolution. Unions were permitted in Stalin's Russia, and strikes were theoretically legal; but in fact they seldom, if ever, occurred.

A democratic society does not want labor disputes settled by revolution. It therefore allows workers and employers to resolve their differences by negotiation and economic pressure, just as it allows buyers and sellers to negotiate the price of an automobile or house. "That government is best which governs least," one of

A bystander is injured during a 1978–79 shipyard strike in Newport ▶ News, Virginia.   UNITED STEELWORKERS OF AMERICA

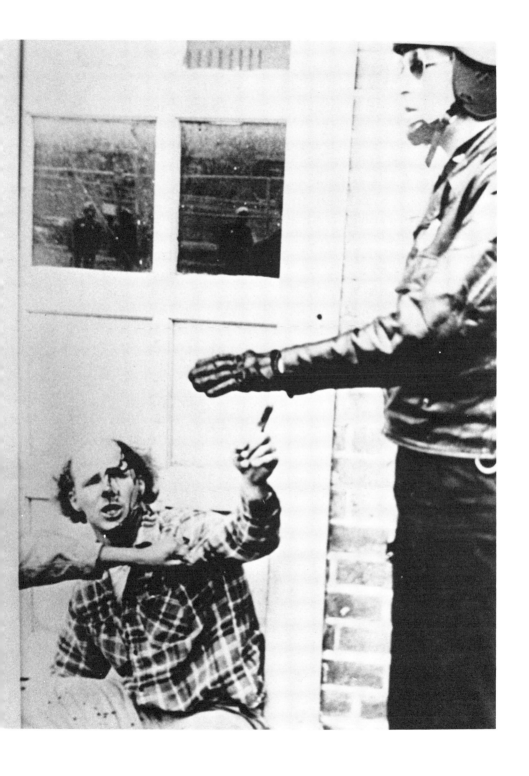

the founders of this country said. If the government were to intervene in all human endeavors, we would indeed be a dictatorship.

"The terms of employment"—wages, hours, and so forth—cannot be made by the government, writes the well-known Wharton School professor, George W. Taylor. Nor should they be, he says, except in special circumstances. "The strike, therefore, is the only available device for inducing the essential compromise and agreement." Employers and unionists "engage in a test of strength," writes E. Wight Bakke of Yale, "for the same reason that nations will go to war: either because it is forced on them, or because they can get what they want in no other way."

In a 1937 decision, Supreme Court Chief Justice Charles Evans Hughes asserted that "long ago we stated the reason for labor organizations . . . that a single employee was helpless in dealing with an employer . . . that union was essential for giving laborers opportunity to deal on an equality with their employers."

Without unions and without the right to strike, the United States would be a totalitarian society.

The aim of a strike is to prevent a company from operating its business—in other words, to reduce its earnings. Unions believe that at a certain point it is cheaper for a company to grant a requested raise or other benefits than to accept the losses of a strike. Management may decide to give in or compromise.

A strike is preceded by negotiations. Either a business agent (the term used for certain officials in the older unions) or an elected committee of rank-and-file workers (in the newer unions) meets with company officials to present demands. The committee may ask, for instance, for a 25 cents-an-hour raise, more vacation pay, and medical insurance. After a number of meetings, the two sides either come to an understanding—let's say for 15 cents an hour and an extra week's vacation—or the union decides that an agreement is not possible and that it must strike to force a settlement.

The issue is then put before a membership meeting of the workers, and the members vote either to accept the company offer or to strike. Usually a majority vote is necessary; in some cases a higher percentage, two-thirds or three-quarters, is required. The Professional Air Traffic Controllers Organization (PATCO) permitted a strike only if 80 percent of the members voted for it. Sometimes the business agent can call a walkout on his own—but this is not the usual practice.

Where a strike involves many plants, say at General Motors or Westinghouse, a representative committee of delegates from each plant is chosen. These delegates may be elected or they may be the officers of the local or national unions.

On the date a strike begins, the union places pickets in front of the plant or store or warehouse being struck. The pickets carry cardboard signs: ON STRIKE AT X COMPANY or HELP US WIN, DON'T GO IN or THIS COMPANY REFUSES TO PAY A LIVING WAGE or THIS COMPANY IS UNFAIR TO ITS EMPLOYEES. The wording on the picket signs varies, limited only by the imagination of those who compose them.

When the pickets are in place, they inform other workers arriving for their usual shift that a strike is on and ask them not to go to work but to join the line instead. In most instances, there are a few scabs—workers who disregard the picket line. The pickets try to dissuade scabs from working by talking to them: "If you go to work, you're only hurting your fellow workers and yourself. Don't you want a raise?" In a few instances, a potential scab may be held back by force. The other main function of pickets is to persuade truck drivers, railroad employees, and others not to make deliveries.

All this sounds nice and calm. The strike changes character, however, if the employer tries to break it. Usually the company will try to get the present working staff to return to the job. A normal technique is for foremen to telephone their workers: "John, why don't you meet me at the corner restaurant. Fifteen other workers are going back to work. We'll have police escort all of you through the picket lines." Usually such strikebreaking efforts are not tried in the first week or two. It is only when the strikers miss a few paychecks and become worried about their families that some may decide to scab.

In another technique, the company hires substitute workers from the outside, and has either police or soldiers escort them through the picket lines. It is much more costly to do this, but management may feel it is cheaper in the long run than giving in to the strikers. Many employers don't resort to such techniques; they feel that the workers will become demoralized after missing five or ten paychecks and come back on their own. The union tries to counteract company strategy by paying strike benefits (usually $25, $50, or $75 a week) to its members—if it has enough money in its treasury.

Those companies that decide to break strikes have done it in many different ways, as we shall soon see. They have done it by using the legal system against strikers; they convince a court, for instance, to declare a strike an illegal conspiracy. Or they prevail on a judge to issue an injunction ordering strikers to reduce their picket lines or remove them entirely. Or they hire private armies of strikebreakers to smash picket lines.

Most of the strikes that have been broken by employers were broken with some form of government help. In theory the government is supposed to be impartial. It doesn't always work out that way.

Which side should fair-minded people take—the strikemakers' or the strikebreakers'? You'll have to decide that for yourself, as we describe numerous strikes and the efforts made to break many of them.

If you put today's labor movement in the context of history, it is well to remember that there were no strikes at all in Colonial days. No one even knew what a strike was. That is because there were very few workers such as those we know today—free workers who have the legal right to quit their jobs.

On the contrary, most of the 3 million Americans who inhabited the thirteen colonies were farmers or tenant farmers who worked for themselves. The rest were black slaves, white slaves, and a small number of masters and journeymen. The farmers and tenant farmers engaged in revolts and rebellions, like Bacon's Rebellion of 1676 in Virginia or the armed uprising of Hudson River Valley tenant farmers in New York in 1766. But those were not strikes of free laborers.

The white slaves (usually called indentured servants, who sold themselves into servitude for seven years—ordinarily to pay for their passage to the colonies) and black slaves also engaged in many revolts and uprisings in the seventeenth and eighteenth centuries. In September 1739, for instance, a sizable group of black slaves attacked an arms magazine near Charleston, South Carolina; killed its two guards; seized weapons; and marched toward Spanish Florida, where the governor promised freedom. On the way, with colors flying and drums beating, they enrolled more recruits, shouted for liberty, and burned everything in their path. Thirty white men were killed (one slave owner was spared because he was said to be kind to his slaves). The revolt failed. Seventy of the black rebels were gibbeted alive. All told there were forty revolts or conspiracies by black slaves in Colonial days, and a lesser number of revolts by white slaves. But those too were not strikes by free workers as we know them today, because slaves did not have the legal right to quit their jobs.

In addition, there were a few skilled craftsmen in Colonial days —carpenters, printers, cabinetmakers, bakers, shoemakers— many of them self-employed. Some went from town to town doing odd jobs. Some were farmers who worked for others in the winter months, then returned home for spring and summer planting. The typical craftsman learned his trade by serving for several years as an apprentice. Then he worked as a journeyman. Finally, if he made a success of it, he became a master, with his own small shop and two or three journeymen.

The journeyman was governed by strict laws and practices. He usually signed a contract to work for a full year. During that time he couldn't quit or be fired. The Colonial government set wages, prices, and standards of quality. It was a crime to earn more than the maximum wage set by law. It was also a crime for laborers to combine—to form a union.

The master wasn't a boss in our sense of the word. He worked side by side with his journeymen and apprentices, with the same elementary tools. There was no division of labor; the master or journeyman made the whole product—say a pair of shoes—all by himself. Nor was there much quarreling over wages, since wages were determined by the price list charged the customer. If that price went up, wages rose apace.

Almost all of the business of the master craftsman was done with people in his own community. A woman would come into the shop of a master shoemaker, for instance, pick out the leather she wanted, discuss the styles, and be measured for size. This was called bespoke work or custom work. There were as yet no retail stores or department stores where you could buy shoes off the shelf. And there was not much competition between masters as to prices and wages, because both of those were set. Consequently, there were no unions and, as far as we know, no strikes.

The Revolution of 1776–83 changed matters. Three things happened. As the nation grew and people moved west and south, the demand for goods increased significantly. Thus, in addition to the master who owned a small shop, there appeared on the scene the merchant-capitalist. The merchant-capitalist produced nothing himself. Instead he bought materials in quantity, sent them out to be fabricated, then sold the finished product to stores, which in turn sold to the public. This was called shopwork—in contrast to bespoke work. The merchant-capitalist never saw the final customer.

Shopwork, produced in large quantities, was of course cheaper than bespoke work. Instead of a single artisan doing the whole job, there was now a tendency to divide the labor into functions. "Cloth must be cheaper made," a seventeenth-century economist wrote, "when one cards, another spins, another weaves, another draws, another dresses, another presses and packs, than when all the operations were performed by the same hand." The merchant-capitalist sought out the cheapest sources of labor—children, women, prisoners sometimes—to keep his costs down and undersell competitors. He also sought out labor-saving machinery when he could.

Ultimately, the new arrangement drove the master craftsman, with his little shop, out of business. It also changed the wage system and laid the basis for labor unions—and strikes. The merchant-capitalist had to compete with other merchant-capitalists, both in his own city and in other cities. He tried to sell more cheaply than his competitors—and keep wages as low as possible. The personal relationship between master and journeyman changed into the more impersonal one between boss and worker. And the two were frequently in conflict—over wages, hours of work, working conditions.

Another change resulted from the industrial revolution, from the introduction of labor-saving machinery. In Britain, James Hargreaves and Richard Arkwright invented the jenny, which could spin hundreds of threads at the same time. Samuel Slater, who had worked for Arkwright in the old country, came here with the plans of the jenny in his head and built a textile mill in Pawtucket, Rhode Island.

Other inventions followed. James Fitch ran a steamboat down the Delaware River. Eli Whitney built a cotton gin that made it possible for one man to do what three hundred workers had done before.

America's whole way of life changed. Factory towns sprang up. Large numbers of people migrated from villages to the cities, and many more came from overseas.

In a typical mill town early in the nineteenth century, the workday was from sunup to 10 P.M. in the summer, a few hours less in the winter. For this, men earned $2.50 to $5.80 a week, depending on their skills; women $2.25; and children under twelve —there were many of them—50 cents a week plus board. Printers, carpenters, shoemakers, and other skilled men fared better, but the feeling of independence was gone. The master craftsman, working on labor-saving machinery, was now a semiskilled operative working for a corporation.

This new state of affairs inevitably caused many disputes—over wages, hours, sanitation, housing. Life became less secure, less pleasant for the new type of laborer than it had been for the farmer and artisan.

There are many advantages to being your own boss. You manage your own affairs. There is pride and challenge in making your own decisions. The person who works for himself sets his own pace, works at times he wants to work, gains satisfaction in making his product, and feels moderately secure. He or she cannot be discharged by someone else or ordered about.

The person who works for someone—particularly if it is an unskilled job—does not have those benefits. He or she cannot ever feel totally secure. If work is slack, the worker can be laid off; and if the worker doesn't satisfy the supervisor, he or she can be fired. There is not the same pride in the work or the same satisfaction in a job well done. The pace of work is set by someone else; so are the hours of work, as well as wages and promotions.

In the new industrial era, the country prospered greatly, but the worker didn't always share in that prosperity. There were frequent periods of economic depression, during which large numbers of people were jobless. There were depressions in 1819, 1837, 1857, 1860, 1873, and so on. Each lasted a few years before prosperity came back, but in the meantime there was unemployment for hundreds of thousands—and soon, millions—of people. Since there was not as yet any such thing as welfare or unemployment compensation, families went hungry.

Commenting on such matters in 1846, a workers' newspaper argued that "the factory system contains in itself the elements of slavery." Laborers often referred to their status as wage slavery.

It was against the evils of wage slavery that the first strikes took place. Fortunately the Bill of Rights guaranteed certain freedoms. Without freedom of speech and freedom of association, unions would have been impossible.

The first unions came into being a decade after the American

Revolution, and they have existed ever since, despite frequent obstacles put in their path and despite thousands of attempts by employers and the government to break strikes.

American unions and strikes were the first in the world, probably because democracy was more developed here than in Britain, France, or anywhere else during most of the nineteenth century.

Oddly enough, there were strikes before there were unions.

No one is exactly sure, but it seems that the first modern-type strike occurred in Philadelphia in 1786. With prices on the rise, printers asked their employers for a wage of $1 a day. When the employers refused, the men struck. After a while, they won their demand. Carpenters in Philadelphia did the same in 1791, in an effort to reduce their work day from 13 hours to 10. The strike soon became a weapon used by other craftsmen—sailors, shoemakers, masons.

Then in 1792, journeymen went a step further; they started to form permanent societies—unions—to press their demands. The first one, that of Philadelphia shoemakers, lasted just one year. But it was reorganized a year later and continued until 1806. These early societies, as they were called, had no full-time representatives or offices and usually lasted a short time. When a worker joined, he took an oath to abide by the society's wage scales, to help other union members find work, and to keep union affairs secret—for fear that employers would discover union plans. It cost 40 or 50 cents to join the union; dues were 6 to 10 cents a month.

The first unions were small groups, limited to a single city, and they almost always went out of existence during a depression or after a defeated strike. In 1809, the Philadelphia Typographical Society had 119 members; the following year it shrank to 55 after it lost a strike. In 1817, the New York Typographical Society had only 84 members, of whom 45 were behind in their dues payments.

Nonetheless, employers offered fierce resistance to these societies and to their strikes. The history of strikemakers and strikebreakers is an interesting one, but the picture is not always pretty.

2 | It's All a Conspiracy

Law? What do I care about law?
Hain't I got the power?
                    Cornelius Vanderbilt

The first major confrontation between strikers and strikebreakers occurred in 1806, in Philadelphia. It was not just a test between workers and employers, but between two opposing factions in the U.S. government—those who supported the philosophy of Alexander Hamilton and those who followed the principles of Thomas Jefferson.

The story begins with the formation of the Federal Society of Journeymen Cordwainers in 1794. A cordwainer was a shoemaker; the word was derived from *cordwain,* a Spanish leather made of goatskin or horsehide, which rich people used for footwear in medieval times. The Philadelphia shoemakers, like most unionists of that period, were highly skilled, and their pay depended on how many pairs of shoes or boots they produced. At the time, it was $2.75 a pair for custom-made boots and $2.50 a pair for boots produced for the retail market. The typical manufactory employed three to twenty journeymen, each supplying his own hand tools, with earnings averaging $6.00 to $11.25 a week.

In forming their union, the shoe workers were following the custom of their bosses. A guild of master shoemakers was organized in Boston as early as 1648. Under a charter granted by the Colony of Massachusetts, the guild in effect enjoyed a monopoly over the production of shoes in the whole colony. If it did not approve of a master shoemaker, he could not operate. If he violated guild rules, he could be fined.

What happened to these early guilds of master craftsmen is not fully recorded. But toward the end of the eighteenth century, Philadelphia employers in the shoe industry formed a Society of Master Cordwainers. Its original purpose, like that of the old guilds, was to guard against unfair competition—masters who charged less or whose costs were less because the work they did was inferior. In due course, the Society of Master Cordwainers added another function—it set the rates paid to workers. Any employer who failed to adhere to these rates was fined.

The journeymen cordwainers who formed their society in 1794 thus were doing something similar—joining together to protect themselves from wage cuts and, if possible, to secure wage increases. The way it worked was simple. The union (society) would meet and set a wage scale—let's say $2.75 for a pair of boots. The scale would be presented to the masters, and if they agreed, that would become the uniform rate throughout Philadelphia.

Any journeyman who worked for a lower scale or refused to join the union was "scabb'd." Other cordwainers would refuse to work in the same shop with him or live in the same boardinghouse. A scab, the cordwainers said, was "a shelter for lice," and they treated human scabs with the same contempt they had for the vermin. Usually this pressure was enough to bring the dissident around; sometimes the employer would fire him rather than lose the rest of his operatives. Unity was the basis of the union's strength.

If the employers rejected the wage scale proposed by the workers or no compromise was reached, the employees would "turn out"—strike. To make sure that every member joined the turnout, the society would hire a picket to go from one shop to another and make sure that no cordwainer was working. In 1798, the owners decided to cut the price paid journeymen for a pair of custom-made boots from $2.75 to $2.25. The employees turned out and succeeded in restoring the old rate.

The following year the employers again tried to cut rates. Again there was a turnout. After nine weeks the strikers won. And so it went. There was a short strike in 1804, which the union won. But after Christmas the employers cut rates by 25 cents a pair.

The workers were unhappy with this reduction but decided to do nothing for the time being. Then in 1805 their society demanded that rates be increased to those prevailing in New York and Baltimore—about 50 cents a pair more. When the employers refused, there was still another turnout. It lasted for six weeks.

This time, however, the employers used a new tactic, designed both to break the strike and prevent unions from ever forming again. They prevailed on the conservative Federalist party, which controlled the local government, to arrest eight strike leaders and charge them with "conspiring" to "increase and augment the prices and rates usually paid and allowed to them"—in other words, with forming a union and trying to get a raise. There had been no violence in the strike, it had been peaceful like the previous ones. But the men were arrested nonetheless, and the effect was to frighten most of the other shoemakers into returning to work. The strike crumbled.

Some months later the government inflicted an even greater blow. The eight strikers were indicted on the charge of having formed "a combination and conspiracy to raise wages." The Federalists stated that this was a violation of British common law, which they said also applied to the United States. Common law is a body of unwritten laws, not passed by any legislature, but based on custom and judicial decisions. In other words, there was no specific statute in Pennsylvania that said it was illegal for a group of workers to ask for a raise, but the Federalists insisted it was unlawful because custom and practice in Britain had so designated it.

The legal arguments actually cloaked a more basic argument. The Federalists, whose leader, Alexander Hamilton, had been killed in 1804 in a duel with Aaron Burr, believed in rapid industrialization and a strong government run by the "rich and well-born." They were also—as might be expected—intensely antilabor. The Democratic-Republican party of Jefferson, on the other hand, was not happy with an industrial system in which children worked 12 or more hours a day. It was distrustful of a strong central government, and believed—as Jefferson had written in the Declaration of Independence—that "all men are created equal." It was natural, therefore, that the Hamiltonians would support the master shoemakers, while the Jeffersonians threw their weight behind the eight strikers who had been arrested.

The indictment caused an uproar in Philadelphia. The Jeffersonian newspaper *Aurora* published an "Address to the Public" by the cordwainers' union, stating that "the name of freedom is but a shadow . . . if we are to be treated as felons and murderers only for asserting the right to take or refuse . . . an adequate reward for our labor." An editorial writer for *Aurora* charged that the employers' use of the conspiracy doctrine was in fact a means "to reduce whites to slavery." There was nothing in either the Constitution of the United States or the Pennsylvania Constitution, he said, "which gave one man a right to say to another what should be the price of his labor."

The cordwainers' strike stirred a bitter controversy. While the eight bootmakers were awaiting trial, the Democratic-Republicans introduced a bill in the Pennsylvania legislature that would have brought the eight unionists instant acquittal. The bill stated that British common law did not apply in Pennsylvania. Had that carried, the indictment against the cordwainers automatically would have become null and void. But the Federalists had the legislative muscle. They defeated the bill by a vote of 44 to 32, and the eight cordwainers were forced to stand trial before a jury of twelve small businessmen and five members of the mayor's court.

It seems remarkable today that anyone could have argued that unions were illegal conspiracies because they sought to raise wages, but that was exactly what prosecutors Joseph Hopkinson and Jared Ingersoll contended. This kind of conspiracy, they said, would interfere with the natural law of supply and demand, would result in higher prices for consumers and hold back the expansion of manufacture in Pennsylvania. They said that if a single worker went on strike—stopped working—in order to pressure his employer into giving him a raise, that was legal. But when two or more did it together, that was a conspiracy in restraint of trade —and a crime. Recorder Moses Levy, a Federalist who sat as judge, called the cordwainers' strike "pregnant with public mischief and private injury." It "tends to demoralize the workmen," he told the jury, and "destroy the trade of the city." It was a wild charge, but it prevailed. The jury found the eight strikers "guilty of a combination to raise their wages," and the court fined them $8 each and ordered them held in jail until the fine was paid. The practical effect was that the cordwainers' union disintegrated.

Based on this case, a number of states adopted the same doctrine—that unions were illegal conspiracies to raise wages. In the next few decades, there were nineteen conspiracy cases against unions in Connecticut, Maryland, Massachusetts, New York, and Pennsylvania. Nonetheless, unions did not disappear. The conspiracy doctrine hobbled them and sometimes led to their dissolution, but other unions appeared in their place. And though unions generally tended to go out of business during depressions, such as the ones of 1819 and 1837, they reappeared when good times returned. Successful strikes for higher wages and shorter hours were engineered by tailors in Buffalo, ship carpenters in Philadelphia, painters and common laborers in New York, cabinetmakers in Baltimore.

Even more, unions began to form unions of unions. In May

1833, Philadelphia carpenters went on strike to increase their daily pay from $1.37 a day to $1.50. When they appealed for help, other craftsmen raised $1,200 for relief funds. After the strike was won, all the unions in the city decided it would be a good idea to set up a city federation of unions. By 1836 there were thirteen such city federations.

In 1834, union people went one step further: They federated the unions of various cities into a National Trades' Union. Before the movement went into steep decline during the depression of 1837, union membership grew from 26,250 to 300,000.

The mood caught on even with women and children. At Lowell, Massachusetts, 2,000 young women went on strike against a 15 percent wage cut. The strike was lost, but two years later, when wages were again reduced—by 12½ percent—the young women went out once more. They sang this song:

> Oh! Isn't it a pity that such a pretty girl as I
> Should be sent to the factory to pine away and die?
> Oh! I cannot be a slave;
> I will not be a slave,
> For I'm so fond of liberty
> That I cannot be a slave.

On July 3, 1835, children at a Paterson, New Jersey, textile mill went on strike to have their hours reduced to 64 a week. With the help of adults, they won a compromise settlement of 69 hours a week.

President Reagan Breaks a Strike

All that harms labor is treason to America. . . .
If any man tells you he loves America, yet he hates
labor, he is a liar. If a man tells you he trusts
America, yet fears labor, he is a fool.
Abraham Lincoln

One hundred and seventy-five years after the Philadelphia court ruled that strikes were illegal combinations and conspiracies, the issue came up again in another form. President Ronald Reagan, in office for only a few months, broke a strike of government employees. He claimed that they had no right to strike.

By this time—1981—almost everyone agreed that workers had the right to form unions and bargain with their employers. In fact a law to that effect, the National Labor Relations Act (also known as the Wagner Act), had been passed in 1935. Under the act, employers were prohibited from firing a worker for joining a union. It may not sound like much of a gain, but many thousands of workers had been fired for just that reason, and many hundreds of strikes had taken place to force companies to sit down with their employees to negotiate wages and working conditions.

Under the new law, employees who petitioned for union recognition were entitled to an election conducted by the National Labor Relations Board (NLRB); and if the union received a majority of the votes, the employer was required to bargain with them. In the fiscal year ending September 30, 1981, the board conducted 7,789 elections, involving 449,243 workers. The unions won almost half those elections. That year the board also ordered that 6,463 workers who were fired for union activity be reinstated to their jobs.

Union leaders criticized the board for long delays and other vices that they said gravely weakened the law. Still, the act established a basic right. Many people referred to the act as labor's Magna Carta, after the document issued by King John of England in 1215, which guaranteed trial by jury and habeas corpus.

Workers not covered by the Wagner Act, however, included government employees—federal, state, and local. Beginning in the 1930s, the number of such employees grew by leaps and bounds (as of 1980 it was 16 million), but they did not have the protection that workers in private industry had.

A change began in 1954, when New York's mayor, Robert Wagner, issued an executive order granting bargaining rights to city employees—if they could show they represented a majority. Under New York rules, a union that represents a specific group of workers, say sanitation workers, applies to the Office of Labor Relations for an election. If it wins, it enters into contract talks with the mayor's committee for collective bargaining, just as in private industry. Under this arrangement, ¼ million New York City employees, ranging from teachers to transport workers, eventually were covered by union agreements.

Then in 1962, President John F. Kennedy issued an order directing executive branch departments to recognize unions if they could prove a majority, and to provide grievance machinery for resolving disputes with them. A grievance, in union terms, is a problem that a worker has with his supervisor. Let's say he is five minutes late to work, but the supervisor docks him thirty minutes' pay. The union takes this up with the government agency, asking for the additional twenty-five minutes' pay.

In the wake of Kennedy's trailblazing act, not only the federal government but twenty-nine states ultimately guaranteed collective bargaining rights. Given this stimulus, the union ranks of government employees grew to almost 4½ million members. More than 1½ million belonged to two teachers' unions, 1 million to a union of state and local workers, ½ million to two general government employees' unions, ⅓ million to police and fire fighters' unions, 1 million to other organizations.

What distressed unionists working for government agencies was that they did not have a legal right to strike. They might talk to government officials about a raise or improvement in conditions, but if no agreement were reached, they had no further recourse. Only eight states permitted any sort of job action by their employees. The rest deemed it a crime, punishable by fines and jail sentences. Under federal law, an employee who went on strike could be sent to jail for a year and fined $1,000.

Fortunately for public employee unions, the law was not strictly enforced. In many instances, leaders of teachers' unions who went on strike were jailed for short periods, but in due course that practice tapered off.

In 1970 a wildcat strike of letter carriers in New York spread to fifteen states and involved 152,100 postal workers. A wildcat strike is one that occurs without the sanction of union officials— in this instance, the head of the letter carriers' union, James Rademacher, pleaded with his members to return to work, but they ignored his pleas. They had lost patience with the government's promises to improve their wage levels, and they were willing to strike even though they faced jail sentences and fines. The government, however, negotiated a new agreement, and no one was fired or imprisoned. Thus, though there were still instances when the federal government did discipline workers who engaged in strikes, the number was relatively small.

It was against this background that a brief but explosive confrontation took place in August 1981 between President Reagan and the Professional Air Traffic Controllers Organization. This union, with some fourteen thousand members nationally, had been formed in 1968 with the help of the well-known attorney, F. Lee Bailey.

The air traffic controllers were men and women who worked in control towers at the nation's airports to guide planes on their landing approaches and takeoffs. Their boss was the federal government, specifically the Federal Aviation Administration (FAA) and the secretary of transportation. And their job was, by everyone's account, most grueling.

The controller sat in front of a scope, watching blips, communicating with pilots on incoming planes, keeping them on separate courses so that they didn't bump into each other. It was nerve-wracking. As Bailey described a scene he witnessed in one tower, "controllers working with 'the picture' on a given scope were forced to eat soup and to urinate into tin cans, because they could not leave their positions. They drank like fish and lived in daily fear of causing midair collision." The salaries of the controllers were considerably above average in 1981: about $30,000 a year base pay, and perhaps $40,000 a year if premium pay for night shifts, weekends, and holidays were included.

On the other hand, as John Thornton, former president of Local 258, the union at the Washington National airport, pointed out, "the washout rate was extremely high." Controllers were required to retire after twenty years, but 90 percent, Thornton says, had to retire earlier because the job was so taxing. Though most of the controllers were young, they had an abnormally high incidence of ailments such as high blood pressure, ulcers, and psychological problems. Hence the main concern of the air controllers had always been to increase the number of persons on the job, lower their hours of work, and make it possible to retire at an earlier age. Dr. Robert Rose, who made a five-year study of air traffic controllers for the FAA, concluded that they were "two or three times more likely than other men their age to develop hypertension—

high blood pressure." PATCO leaders pointed out that the 40-hour week for air controllers was longer than that of controllers in other major industrial countries. It was also much longer than that of pilots, who work under similar tensions.

Until the strike of 1981, PATCO had been singularly unsuccessful in remedying this state of affairs. Not long after the organization was formed, controllers in the Northeast conducted a slowdown to put pressure on the government. By strictly following all rules, they took much more time than usual to bring in each plane and consequently snarled traffic at every major airport in the area. In 1970, controllers conducted a sick-in—they called in sick and stayed home. The FAA fired 60 of the 2,319 controllers involved, but later rehired all but 1. Perhaps the administration backtracked because federal judge George Hart ruled that the sick-in was the result of "extreme provocation" by the FAA. No further strikes or slowdowns took place for the next few years.

In 1980, PATCO's leadership had cause to rejoice—or at least thought it did. Republican presidential candidate Ronald Reagan had taken a sympathetic interest in their cause. Robert E. Poli, president of PATCO, met with candidate Reagan in Tampa, Florida, and on October 20 Reagan sent Poli a formal letter promising to "take whatever steps are necessary to provide our air traffic controllers with the most modern equipment available and to adjust staff levels and workdays." Poli was so elated with Reagan's pledge of cooperation that he urged the union to endorse the former California governor for president. Indeed PATCO was one of only three unions that supported the Republican candidate. In a sense, it put all its eggs in Reagan's basket, hoping to achieve through him what it had been unable to achieve in a dozen years of negotiations, pleading, and sick-ins.

The old contract between PATCO and the Federal Aviation Administration was set to expire in March 1981. Negotiations for a new one began in February, shortly after Reagan took the oath of office. The union made three major demands—a reduced workweek of 32 hours, an improved retirement plan, and a wage increase. The FAA said that the total cost would be about $600 million a year, far beyond what it was prepared to spend. It refused to make any concessions on the item that troubled the controllers most—the length of their workweek.

There was an interesting aspect to this confrontation. President Reagan was in the process of drastically reducing social expenditures—for welfare, food stamps, public housing, aid to education, even children's lunches—in order, he said, to balance the national budget. He and his secretary of transportation, Drew Lewis, undoubtedly felt it would be out of character, therefore, to significantly increase spending for air controllers. A couple of million other government employees—who were being asked to take relatively small raises—would be upset if the skilled and highly paid controllers were to get a much better deal. Making promises during an election campaign was one thing; facing the real problems of government after the election was something else.

President Reagan and Secretary Lewis took a tough stand. They were willing to grant a raise of about $4,000 a year for each controller, but no more. John Thornton says that "wages were not our big issue; we wanted a shorter work schedule so that we could take some of the tension out of our job."

Why the FAA and Secretary Lewis did not respond to that concern is not clear. Perhaps they felt that if the workweek were reduced, they would have to train many new controllers to take up the slack. The training was both long and expensive. Perhaps they were afraid that adding many new men and women would reduce efficiency. In any case, they refused to yield.

On the union's side, the controllers felt that the president was reneging on a solemn promise. They also were confident that when a strike became imminent, the government would back off. To add a little pressure on the FAA, the union engaged in "informational picketing." Workers didn't strike, but in their nonworking hours they carried picket signs at the air terminals and gave leaflets to the public explaining what they wanted, and why.

The tactic didn't help. PATCO and the government were

headed for a showdown. The union delayed a strike in June because only 75 percent of its members voted to walk off the job, and the union's constitution stated that at least 80 percent must do so. Poli thereupon signed the contract offered by the Reagan administration and submitted it to a vote of the membership. Ninety-five percent rejected it. Though there were some meetings with the government afterward and a few minor changes in the offer, a strike was inevitable. More than the required 80 percent now favored one. On August 3, 1981, the strike began—12,700 of the 16,000 air controllers walked off the job. Most of them expected the strike to be short and sweet.

Had PATCO gone on strike when the old contract expired, the controllers might have fared better. March was a bad weather month, requiring the greatest skill of the air traffic controllers. Unskilled substitutes would have been a decided handicap. There was also the fact that Congress was in session then and might have exerted some pressure on President Reagan to compromise. A majority of the House of Representatives, after all, were members of the opposition Democratic party. August, by contrast, was a poor month to strike—many business people who used airlines regularly were on vacation, the weather was good, and Congress was in recess.

President Reagan took a surprisingly tough stand on the work stoppage. Only hours after it began, he went on television to warn the strikers that if they didn't return to work within 48 hours, they would be fired. That's the kind of threat many employers make during a strike; in most instances, it is forgotten once the strike is settled. But in this case President Reagan refused to back off. He said the controllers had broken their pledge not to strike—a pledge each was required to sign on being hired. The president argued that it was permissible for "workers in the private sector to strike" but "we cannot compare labor-management relations in the private sector with the government." Commenting on the president's point, teachers' union president Albert Shanker stated: "It's strange that the United States, which got rid of King George

Members of the Professional Air Traffic Controllers Organization raise clenched fists in front of Chicago's O'Hare airport control tower in response to President Reagan's demand that air traffic controllers return to work.   AP/WIDE WORLD PHOTOS

III over two hundred years ago, is about the only democracy still saddled with the notion from old monarchial days that any public 'servant' who strikes is really engaged in a rebellion against the sovereign and therefore must be severely punished."

President Reagan's punishment was swift and devastating. On August 5, he ordered the FAA to send letters to each of the 12,700 strikers, telling them they were fired and would not be rehired. Some strikers did return to work in the 48-hour grace period given them by the president, but 11,600 stayed out to the end. The discharge notices were followed by a blizzard of court actions. Almost immediately after the walkout, the government sought and was granted fifty-two separate court decrees ordering the controllers back to work. It was impossible, of course, to put 11,600 people in jail for defying those orders, but 5 PATCO leaders were imprisoned, and 7 or 8 more were subsequently given contempt sentences of ten to ninety days. Judges imposed fines on the union totalling $32 million. They froze the union's $3.5 million strike fund, thus preventing PATCO from giving financial aid to its members.

In addition, the government petitioned the Federal Labor Relations Authority for decertification of PATCO. The authority, whose functions are similar to those of the National Labor Relations Board, is empowered to grant collective bargaining rights after an election—and also to take them away if it sees fit. In this instance it took them away—it decertified the union, in effect putting it out of business. The president stuck to his threat. He had said he would fire every striker, and he did. As of 1984, only a handful were allowed to return. President Reagan also said he would not enter into further negotiations with PATCO, and he maintained his position on that as well.

The American Federation of Labor and Congress of Industrial Organizations (AFL-CIO) tried to help PATCO. Behind the scenes, it pressured the president to accept mediation of the dispute. Liberals of all types, in and out of the labor movement, spoke out in favor of a compromise. It became obvious almost at once, however, that PATCO had been trigger-happy. The strike may have been justified, but the leadership of the union made little effort to line up the support of other unions or the public in advance. If it could have secured assurances that the pilots who flew the planes, the mechanics who serviced them, and the flight attendants who served the customers would honor PATCO picket lines, the administration probably would have had to retreat.

But the PATCO leadership didn't bother to arrange for that kind of help. The pilots' union, a conservative organization, probably would not have helped in any case. Other unions might have, however. And the public too could have been enlisted in PATCO's cause. Unfortunately PATCO was conceived of as a haughty group of overpaid people; and since it made little effort to change that image, it won few friends. PATCO's leaders believed that commercial airplanes could not operate without PATCO members at the control towers.

They were proven wrong.

The Federal Aviation Administration immediately enlisted supervisors, instructors, retired controllers, and five hundred military air traffic specialists to work the radarscopes. In addition, there were a few thousand controllers who had either refused to strike or who had gone back within the first 48 hours. The airports were able to continue service—though very inadequately. With a staff of only five thousand persons, air traffic at the twenty-two major airports had to be cut by 50 percent, and private airplane traffic even more drastically. In fifty-eight communities, the FAA closed down control towers entirely.

The government planned to train eight thousand new controllers. The course, given in Oklahoma City, would take seventeen weeks and was expensive, costing the government $175,000 per trainee. Quite a few trainees flunked out. According to the Democratic Study Group of the House of Representatives, the price tag for training alone would be $1.4 billion. Totalling these costs along with the losses to businesses, airlines, cities, and airports, the total damage to the economy ran into billions.

The Reagan administration, however, persevered. It broke the PATCO strike and put the union out of business, just as the Philadelphia court put the cordwainers' union out of business in 1806.

Some air traffic controllers found other jobs in the airline industry. Most were out of work for a long time and then had to look elsewhere. With PATCO dissolved, the controllers formed another union, the United States Air Traffic Controllers Organization (USATCO), to press the claim for their old jobs. Perhaps they will ultimately recover from President Reagan's strikebreaking.

But many say they will not. It was the most staggering defeat federal workers have ever suffered in this country.

The Molly Maguires

Theirs was a barbarous protest against barbarity.
Herbert Harris,
writing about the Molly Maguires

No one was killed in the shoemakers' strike of 1805 or in the air controllers' strike of 1981. That was generally true of strikes that occurred from 1794 to the Civil War and from 1939 to the present. But in the seven decades from 1870 to 1939, thousands of workers were killed and wounded in the course of work stoppages, and scores of thousands jailed.

It was a period of violence, between strikers on the one hand and employers and the government on the other, such as the nation had never seen before or since. The New York *Tribune* of 1877 called the railroad strike of that year a labor war, an apt term for almost all of the major strikes in the ensuing decades. They were just that—little wars.

Outlook magazine in 1904 made a study of strikes and strikebreaking during a period of thirty-three months. It found that 198 pickets had been killed; 1,966 wounded; 6,114 arrested. The number of strike-related deaths in this short period was about half what the United States suffered in the Spanish-American War; the number of wounded was slightly higher than American casualties in that war. And this was for a period of less than three years!

What caused the labor wars? You could call it immaturity—unions and employers (and the government) had not yet learned how to deal with each other. Or you could call it greed; there was an enormous surge in business, but management was not willing to share its profits fairly with working people—especially the large group of foreign immigrants who came to the United States after the Civil War. Whatever the cause, it brought in its wake immeasurable suffering.

One of the groups that had more than its share of labor wars was the coal miners. Not much coal was used in the early days of America. Farmers preferred wood for their fireplaces, and iron manufacturers preferred charcoal. From 1808 to 1820, only twelve thousand tons of coal were mined. But in 1833, Frederick W. Geisenheimer took out a patent for smelting iron with anthracite coal, and soon coal mining turned into a large-scale industry in an area of eastern Pennsylvania 120 miles by 50 miles. By 1840, production of the precious fuel had grown to a million tons a year, and just before the Civil War, to eight and a half million tons. It was a typical American success story.

In step with this expansion, Welsh, English, German, and Irish settlers converged on the five anthracite counties of eastern Pennsylvania to find work. The Irish were the largest of these groups —and by far the most abused. Two million of them had fled to America in the first half of the nineteenth century, 1.2 million from 1846 to 1854 alone. Being unskilled, they had to take menial jobs on turnpikes and canals, sometimes far from their families, at wages as low as 62, 75, or 87 cents a day. Hundreds died annually from the illnesses of poverty, such as tuberculosis. Yet, because these immigrants were so spirited and fought against injustice so militantly, many employers didn't want to hire them. In their want ads, employers sometimes inserted the clause: Irish need not apply.

It was no wonder then that many Irishmen sought work in the mines of Schuylkill and its neighboring counties in the anthracite area, and that they were willing to work under harsh conditions. At the center of their lives was the company—the mining company that owned the mine, the land, the streets, and usually the little three-room apartments lacking plumbing or other amenities, in which they were housed.

The streets were patrolled by company police; the local store was owned by the company; the doctor who brought children into the world was a company doctor; the church and school were run by men who did the company's bidding. If you didn't shop at the company store or if you were a troublemaker, there was a good chance you would be fired.

Mining itself was terribly unpleasant and unsafe. Workers spent hours stooped in the damp and smelly air below ground and were subject to all kinds of health hazards—noxious fumes such as stinkdamp, rotten gas, carbon monoxide, and coal dust, which caused bronchial catarrh. The rate of accidents from explosions, falling rock, fire, and suffocation was far greater than in other industries. In one seven-year period, 566 miners were killed and 1,655 injured in Schuylkill County alone. Tens of thousands of men worked in semidarkness, sometimes knee-deep in water, always in fear of cave-ins or explosions. As one mining clerk put it, their lot was "little better than semislavery." One-quarter of them were children age seven to sixteen, paid $1 to $3 a week to separate coal from slate as it came down the chutes.

In this unhappy situation, the Irish miners sought help and protection, trying to claw their way up through mutual aid societies, unions, and politics. The Ancient Order of Hibernians (AOH), to which thousands of the Irish flocked, was the largest mutual aid society in the nation at the time. Its stated purpose was to "promote friendship, unity, and true Christian charity among the members." Among its tasks were raising money to aid "the aged, sick, blind, and infirm members" and acting as a gathering place for parties and social activities.

Like many other such organizations at the time—including

unions such as the Knights of St. Crispin or the Knights of Labor —the AOH adopted secret rituals and passwords that lent an air of mystery to it. The organization was also the meeting ground for Irish miners who wanted to form unions (as most of them did) or beat up particularly unjust foremen. In time these militant members of the Hibernians were dubbed "Molly Maguires" by the mining companies and the Pinkerton Detective Agency, which was hired by the companies to spy on the miners. Legend has it that the Mollies were named after a widowed Irish lady in Ballymena, County Antrim, who in 1839 fought off bailiffs trying to evict her from her home. But there is considerable doubt that there ever was any miners' group in the United States that called itself the Molly Maguires; more likely it was a sarcastic name given to AOH members who challenged the coal operators.

In any case, the Molly Maguires were quick to use physical violence against company supervisors who tormented them. In 1862, F. W. Langdon, a mine foreman who supposedly was guilty of short-weighing (giving the miners credit for less coal than they actually mined), was beaten and stoned at a Fourth of July celebration in Carbon County; he died the next day. A mineowner named George K. Smith, hated for similar reasons by the miners, was shot through the head by a group of men with blackened faces, while his family looked on in horror.

Murders were carefully planned, often committed by an AOH member from another county. From January 1, 1860, to April 1, 1867, according to a tally by the *Miners' Journal,* at least sixty-three unsolved murders took place in eastern Pennsylvania, most of them acts of vengeance against mineowners and their supervisors. There were, in addition, many times that number of threats. Typically, a penciled note with a rough picture of a coffin and a pistol was delivered to a mine boss. It read: We will give you one week to go, but if you are alive on next Saturday, you will die.

This was a period when unionism in the coal field was temporarily on the wane. It revived in 1867 when a talented immigrant named John Siney led a small strike of four hundred diggers at the Eagle Colliery in protest against a 10 percent wage cut. By a stroke

A meeting of the Molly Maguires, militant coal miners who often used violence to resolve disputes with mine owners   LIBRARY OF CONGRESS

of good fortune, the strike was successful and the cut rescinded. Siney was able to bring together a number of local union groups to form the Workingmen's Benevolent Association (WBA), with himself as president. The WBA soon had thirty thousand members, four-fifths of the miners in the Pennsylvania anthracite region.

From 1868 to 1875, it was a race between the union—the WBA —and the coal industry, which was increasingly being taken over by the railroads. There were strikes almost every year. The first one, in 1868, was for shorter hours—an 8-hour workday. It was defeated. The next year there was an accident at the Avondale mine in Luzerne County, where 109 miners died. Addressing the thousands of mourners who came to the funeral, Siney said, "Men, if you must die with your boots on, die for your families, your homes, your country, but do not longer consent to die like rats in a trap for those who have no more interest in you than in the pick you dig with."

That same year the miners struck against a wage cut and succeeded in getting a written contract for the first time, with a sliding scale of wages—if the price of coal went up, so did wages; if it went down, wages too fell. The agreement, however, brought no peace. The Anthracite Board of Trade tried each year to reduce the rates, and each year the union resisted. A strike in 1870 lasted six months; one in 1875, five months. Neither was a success; in fact, the latter was a bitter defeat for the miners. Siney, however, did win some favorable laws from the Pennsylvania legislature, including one that gave workers the right to form unions and revoked the old conspiracy doctrine. (Siney himself was indicted for conspiracy in 1875.) Mine inspection bills were also passed, after the disastrous accident at the Avondale mine. These political gains were modest, but they gave the miners hope for the future.

One man was intensely determined, however, to demolish both the union and the Molly Maguires. His name was Franklin Benjamin Gowen. He was a young, clean-shaven, second generation Irish American whose father had made a fortune selling groceries and liquor. Gowen himself enjoyed a sensational career in law and politics, emerging at age thirty-three as the president of the Philadelphia and Reading Railroad, popularly known as the Reading.

Gowen was typical of a group of business people of that era whom historians have called the robber barons. Like Jay Gould and Cornelius Vanderbilt, who used unethical means to carve out empires in the railroad industry, Gowen used his control of the Reading Railroad to dominate the coal industry. Since all coal had to be shipped by barge or rail—more and more of it by rail—Gowen had great leverage in gaining control of the anthracite industry.

He formed a mineowners' association called the Anthracite Board of Trade. Like the Society of Master Cordwainers almost a century earlier, Gowen's organization sought to control both the price of coal to the retailer and the wage rates of coal miners. If any owner refused to accept his terms, Gowen would raise shipping charges or refuse to ship the coal altogether. By this technique, from 1871 to 1874 the Reading Railroad was able to buy a hundred thousand acres of coal lands in the southern sector of the anthracite region, and to dominate the industry.

Gowen also cut the union down to size. A typical situation was the way he forced employers and workers to abide by his decisions. In January 1871, miners of the northern part of the anthracite area downed tools—went on strike—because the owners had reduced wages by one-third. Miners in the southern area joined their northern brethren, and the strikers entertained high hopes of success.

Since this was the third strike in three years, by February both the men and the owners were hurting badly. "Men, women, and children are suffering from lack of clothing and food," reported the *Miners' Journal.* Many children, it said, were dying.

On the other side, a number of independent mineowners were near bankruptcy, and several had agreed to reopen their shafts on the union's terms. Gowen, however, would not permit it. Those owners who were willing to bargain with the Workingmen's Benevolent Association were told that freight costs would double— from $2 a ton to $4. Such manipulation of the anthracite economy terrified pro-management sources. "If a railroad company can advance or lower its charges for transportation at will, there is not an industrial operation that may not be destroyed in a month," said the Harrisburg *State Journal.* The parties eventually agreed to arbitration, but the arbitrator cut minimum wages and ruled that union miners could no longer refuse to work with nonunion men—a ruling that weakened the WBA appreciably.

In 1873—a year of severe economic depression—Gowen took two steps to tighten his control of the industry. At his initiative, railroad owners held a secret meeting in New York and agreed on a fixed price of $5 a ton for coal. They also divided the market among six companies, with Gowen's Reading Railroad receiving the largest share, almost 28 percent. There were as yet no antitrust laws in the United States to rule such collusion illegal, as would be the case today. It is interesting that the corporations took concerted action to improve their own position, but were hostile to the miners for trying to do the same thing with their union.

The second step taken by Gowen was to hire a detective named Allan Pinkerton to smash the Molly Maguires, the radical wing of the union. Some of the Mollies, like Thomas Munley, had fought for liberty in Ireland and seen some of their friends hanged for wearing of the green. They were a thorn in Gowen's side. Unlike Siney, who now was advocating arbitration rather than strikes as a means of settling disputes with the coal companies, the Mollies insisted on more militant action.

Pinkerton was just the man for the job. An immigrant from Scotland and a former radical himself, he had been in the detective business for a long time. But his agency was in such severe straits during the depression of 1873, he was afraid it would go bankrupt. Paid $100,000 by Gowen and his associates, Pinkerton insinuated dozens of spies into the union's ranks. Today that would be illegal, but in 1873 there were no laws protecting unions from such deviltry. One of the spies, P. M. Cummings, became an official of the WBA and a close associate of Siney's.

The most effective Pinkerton agent, it turned out, was James McParlan, a twenty-nine-year-old native of Ireland, who assumed the name James McKenna. A charming extrovert, with red hair and a fine tenor voice, McParlan danced a tolerable jig, told a smutty story, drank with the best of them, and used his fists handily. Posing as a counterfeiter and a murderer on the lam, McParlan passed himself off as a member of the AOH from another section of the country and was duly initiated into the Shenandoah Lodge of AOH, which had two hundred members. He traveled widely, seeking evidence of murder plots, always flashing a big bankroll and buying drinks.

Meanwhile the union was preparing for still another strike, and Gowen was preparing to break it; this time, he hoped, he would smash the union forever. He hired still more spies and increased production so that there would be a stockpile of coal aboveground to meet public demand for a long time. In December 1874, Gowen and the other owners reduced wages by 10 to 20 percent. According to the *Miners' Journal,* however, wages were of secondary importance; Gowen was bent on "disbanding of the Miners' and Laborers' Benevolent Association," formerly called the Workingmen's Benevolent Association.

In a subsequent report to his stockholders, Gowen admitted he spent $4 million to break the strike—called the long strike because it lasted for five months. It was worth every penny, he said, because it saved the company "from the arbitrary control of an irresponsible trades union." During the strike, two squadrons of agents were organized: one headed by a Pinkerton agent named Robert J. Linden and the other by Captain W. J. Heisler, whose purpose was to attack strikers physically and make it possible for strikebreakers to take their places. The existing coal and iron police force was expanded, and a vigilance committee was formed, which, in Pinkerton's words, was "to take fearful revenge on the Molly Maguires."

Gowen got what he bargained for, especially as the months ticked by and the miners became more desperate. "Hundreds of families," reported Andrew Roy, a contemporary, "rose in the morning to breakfast on a crust of bread and a glass of water, who did not know where a bite of dinner was to come from. Day after day, men, women, and children went to the adjoining woods to dig roots and pick up herbs to keep body and soul together." Meanwhile they watched grimly as the operators recruited strikebreakers to take their jobs, and unleashed the coal and iron police to maim and kill active strikers.

In March 1885, Edward Coyle, a union leader and AOH chief, was murdered at the Plank Colliery, which belonged to the Reading. Another AOH activist was killed by a mine engineer at Mine Hill Gap. One mine boss, Patrick Vary, shot indiscriminately into a group of three hundred strikers, leaving, as Gowen later said, "a long trail of blood behind them." Vary was never brought to trial. Vigilantes and a mine boss fired their guns at a hundred miners in Tuscarora, killing one digger and wounding others. One assailant was arrested and tried, but found not guilty on the ground that he was protecting himself. Colliery foremen, as well as strikebreakers and such hoodlum gangs as the Modocs, were given guns by the operators to brandish at strikers.

The coal diggers responded in kind. Strikebreakers were sometimes found dead in ditches. Hungry and desperate, the miners chased the "blacklegs," calling them traitors and beating them whenever they could find them. The strikers were determined to hold out, as evidenced by this song they composed:

> Now two long months are nearly over—
>   that no one can deny,
> And for to stand another
>   we are willing for to try,
> Our wages shall not be reduced,
>   tho' poverty do reign,
> We'll have seventy-four basis, boys,
>   before we work again.

On June 3, a crowd gathered at Glover's Hill opposite a colliery still in production, determined to pull the scabs out. They were met by Gowen's agents Linden and Heisler and 24 armed men. In the strikers' group were 613 miners, with the Pinkerton spy McParlan in the vanguard—shouting and screaming, two pistols in his belt and his bulldog by his side. The rest of the miners evidently had no weapons, for they backed away to another area, where they put three collieries out of production. Then, joined by strikers from Hazleton who had also closed down a few pits, they moved toward another colliery. Here, however, they came eye to eye with the state militia that Governor John F. Hartranft had ordered out. In the face of such overwhelming force, the miners dispersed. This was typical of events throughout the strike.

Gowen later listed ninety-two separate instances of worker assault, arson, murder, riots, and destruction of property. J. Walter Coleman, in his book *The Molly Maguire Riots,* printed thirteen full pages about the acts of violence on both sides, ranging from

"Blacklegs," or strikebreakers, are jeered during a coal miners' strike.

the burning of a telegraph office at a railroad station to the derailing of trains, dumping of coal cars, beatings, threats, and a few actual murders. But many, if not most, of the illegal acts were perpetrated by agents of the owners, according to Marvin W. Schlegel, a historian who wrote a favorable biography of Gowen. "The facts," he said, "show that there was much more terror waged against the Mollies than those illiterate Irishman ever aroused."

After five months, the strikers were at last forced to give up. Short of money and food, and drained by strikes in previous years, they could no longer hold out. "Since I last saw you," a striker wrote to a friend, "I have buried my youngest child, and on the day before his death there was not one bit of victuals in the house with six children."

The corporations began reopening their pits toward the end of May, offering police protection to those willing to cross picket lines. On June 8, the union's executive board made a final, desperate plea to Gowen for a compromise. He turned them down. On June 14, the union gave up: "We can continue the fight no longer." One of their local leaders, a Civil War veteran named John Walsh, admitted, "We are beaten, forced by the unrelenting necessities of our wives and little ones to accept terms which . . . we could never under any other circumstances have been forced to accept." The most active strikers were placed on a blacklist—a list of miners who were never to be rehired by the owners under any circumstances. Others returned to work on Gowen's terms, their wages cut by 20 percent.

Like a dam that breaks, however, the defeated strike brought in its wake a further wave of violence and bitterness. Irish miners, now without a union, fought back with their own two fists—and sometimes with stronger weapons. Foremen on the company side were furnished guns with which to threaten their men. On more than one occasion, miners were shot dead, usually by parties unknown. On December 1, 1875, at Wiggan's Patch, near Mahanoy City, for instance, terrorists invaded the home of Charles O'Donnell while his family was sleeping. O'Donnell and one of his boarders fled, but were captured and killed. O'Donnell had fourteen bullets in his body.

With the strike over, James McParlan's two years of espionage activities were put to greater use. He compiled a list of AOH members—347 names in all—including 14 who were described as murderers and accessories accused of killing various people. A number of Mollies were arrested and charged with capital crimes.

The first trial of the accused began in Mauch Chunk in January

1876. But the proceedings in May received the greatest publicity. Five so-called Mollies were accused of killing policeman Benjamin F. Yost on July 5 the year before, while he was putting out a gas lamp near his home at Tamaqua. As the trial opened, Gowen himself appeared in court as a special prosecutor. He dominated the trial, as he dominated the coal and rail industries of his area. At Gowen's command, a few of the defense witnesses were arrested as they left the stand and charged with perjury.

McParlan, of course, was the main prosecution witness; he was almost the whole case in fact. He claimed that the five men had all confessed to him that they had killed Yost. The trial was notable for the weakness of prosecution evidence. For instance, one witness said he had seen union leader Thomas Munley kill a mine foreman named Thomas Sanger. When Munley was asked to stand, the witness said, "This is not the man." Yet Munley was convicted and hanged. One after another, in various trials, nineteen men were found guilty and executed. Others were given prison terms.

June 21, 1877, was called Pennsylvania's Day With the Rope. On that day, ten miners, allegedly members of the Molly Maguires and convicted as murderers, were executed. First to mount the double gallows were James Boyle, an American-born miner who had worked for five years at the Number 5 Colliery in the Panther Creek valley, and Hugh McGeehan, a young Irishman who had been blacklisted by the coal owners for his role in the long strike of 1875. "Good-bye, old fellow," Boyle said to McGeehan, "we'll die like men." In McGeehan's buttonhole were two roses, one pink and one white. In one hand he held a brass crucifix; in the other, a porcelain statuette of the Blessed Virgin. Boyle carried a huge red rose, which fell to the ground as the trap was sprung.

Next to be brought to the scaffold were a forty-year-old tavern owner, secretary of the Tamaqua AOH, and a younger man, a recent arrival from Ireland. Two more men were executed that day in the jail yard at Pottsville, and four more at Mauch Chunk —all Hibernians and all presumably Molly Maguires. Nine more were executed later, the last two in January 1879, only a few minutes before a letter arrived from the governor—too late of course—commuting their sentences to life imprisonment.

After the first hangings, the Philadelphia *Times* carried a big headline, Justice at Last. The Chicago *Tribune* made a similar point: A Triumph of Law and Justice. One coal owner's paper, analyzing the crime of the Mollies, described it this way: "Whenever prices of labor did not suit them, they organized and proclaimed a strike."

But workers took an opposite tack. In New York a protest meeting was held. The group adopted a resolution denouncing the testimony of the stool pigeon McParlan, and accused the operators of trying to divert "attention from their own cruel and outrageous robbery of the workmen." Demonstrators in Philadelphia decried "the hasty and inhuman manner in which the so-called Molly Maguires have been sentenced to death."

After the last execution, a New York *World* reporter wrote: "The demeanor of the men on the scaffold, their resolute and yet quiet protestations of innocence . . . were things to stagger one's belief in their guilt. . . . They were arrested and arraigned at a time of great public excitement, and they were condemned and hanged on 'general principles.' "

Two Weeks of Insurrection

So long as they can do my work for what I choose to pay them, I keep them, getting out of them all I can. . . . They must look out for themselves, as I do for myself. When my machines get old and useless, I reject them and get new ones, and these people are part of my machinery.

nineteenth-century New England mill owner

Mark Twain called the period after the Civil War the Gilded Age. New industries mushroomed as never before, and some men (and a few women) made unbelievable fortunes. This is the way Louis Adamic described the period in his book *Dynamite*:

The competitive spirit grew fiercer every year. It was the beginning of relentless business methods; of secret rates and rebates, graft, subterranean intrigue, murder, special legislation passed by bought lawmakers. . . . It was industrial and financial anarchy, exuberant, hard, irresistible. The Constitution of the United States passed for a joke, and so did the presidency and the Supreme Court. . . . The Federal government became . . . virtually the Central Office of Big Business.

Jay Gould and Cornelius Vanderbilt were symbols of the time. Gould began his career by cheating two partners in a leather factory. Later he made a fortune manipulating stocks on the New York Stock Exchange. In 1867, at the age of thirty-two, he printed and sold counterfeit shares of stock in the Erie Railroad. When the fraud was discovered in New York, Gould and his partner, Jim Fisk, slipped away to New Jersey with $6 million in cash and the Erie financial records. Later he bribed New York legislators to make his fraud legal.

Vanderbilt built an empire out of a hundred dollars he borrowed from his mother in 1801 to buy a barge. When he moved from shipping to railroads many years later, he gained control of the New York Central by forcing its customers to slosh through two miles of snow and mud at East Albany to make connections with his own Hudson Railroad, which would take them to New York City. By thus depressing the value of New York Central's stock, he was able to buy a controlling interest for $18 million, and after bribing a number of state legislators, he was permitted to merge it with his own railroad. At that point, Vanderbilt watered the stock by $44 million. That means he issued $44 million more in shares than the value of all New York Central's property. His personal profit was $26 million—$6 million in cash and $20 million in stock—an incredible return for a single operation.

The point about men like Gould and Vanderbilt was that they had nothing to do with developing the industries that made them rich. They invented nothing. They reaped the reward for what others had done. Their knack was for manipulating money and conceiving shady deals.

While the United States was experiencing unparalleled growth, it was also experiencing an orgy of corruption and thievery. Typical was a transaction by J. P. Morgan, which launched him on his financial career. Morgan bought defective rifles—already condemned—from the government for $17,500, then sold them the very next day to the same government for $110,000. Helped by congressmen whom they had bribed, three western railroads were given not only federal loans for each mile of track but outright gifts of 70 million acres. A railroad construction company, the Credit Mobilier Company of America, headed by a member of Congress, Oakes Ames, swindled the government out of $44 million while building the Union Pacific Railroad. Ames spread around $436,000 in bribes where it would "do the most good," and promised instant wealth to a number of insiders, such as the future candidate for president, Senator James G. Blaine, and a future president, James A. Garfield. Some of Ames's colleagues in the House received free stock—stock that paid a dividend of 625 percent in a single year!

Though some railmen, such as James J. Hill of the Great Northern, performed valuable services for the farmers—such as finding foreign markets for them—a majority were interested only in growing rich. In Kansas, $300 million of stock certificates were issued to build eight thousand miles of rail, even though the cost was just $100 million. A financial newspaper noted in 1869 that twenty-eight corporations had hiked their capital value 40 percent in two years. It was not for naught that the heads of the railroads were called robber barons. The moral tone of the Gilded Age was indicated by Vanderbilt when he shouted, "What do I care about law? Hain't I got the power?"

The Gilded Age was a period of wild growth—and extremes of both wealth and poverty. From 1850 to 1900 the population of the United States tripled—from 23 million to 76 million. From just before the Civil War until the end of World War I, the value of manufactured goods skyrocketed by thirty-three times. Small industries, some of which hadn't even existed before the Civil War, grew immense—coal, steel, railroads, farm equipment, metal mining; and men who used to consider a hundred thousand or two hundred thousand dollars a great fortune now measured their wealth in millions and tens of millions.

On the other side of the social scale were the poor, a large number of them immigrants. The cities were filled with foreign-born, many of whom couldn't speak English. In 1860, 47 percent of the population of New York City was composed of immigrants,

50 percent of Chicago, 29 percent of Philadelphia, and 60 percent of Saint Louis. Men and women of different nationalities could easily be pitted against one another. When a strike took place, an employer could hire people of one nationality to break the strike of another, or import laborers from Europe. Moreover, living in a strange land, unacquainted with its culture and habits, the immigrants were easy prey for unscrupulous employers. They worked in sweatshops under poor conditions of health and safety, received low wages, and were usually afraid to form unions for fear of being discharged.

The industrialists of the post–Civil War period were often ruthless in dealing with their workers, especially in periods of economic downturn. Nowhere was this more evident than in the railroad industry, the fastest growing and most important industry of the time. It resulted in two nationwide strikes—in 1877 and 1894—and for the first time involved the U.S. government itself as the primary strikebreaker.

The main means of transport in early America was by road or waterway. But in 1804, an inventor named Oliver Evans put a steam engine on wheels (later known as the iron horse) and drove it on hard ground through Philadelphia. Then in 1818, another inventor, John Stevens, drove the "steamboat on wheels" over a narrow-gage track on his estate in Hoboken, New Jersey.

In Britain in 1829, George Stephenson's locomotive *Rocket* dragged a thirteen-ton train over tracks at the amazing speed of fifteen miles an hour. Though there were doubts originally that the railroad would ever compete with canals as a means of transportation, it soon proved to be much better; it was quicker and able to reach almost anywhere.

By 1830, the first modern railroad, the Baltimore & Ohio (B & O), had been completed. It shipped goods from Baltimore to Ellicott's Mills thirteen miles away. Soon charters were granted to companies that would eventually become the New York Central and Pennsylvania systems. And railroads changed, from being feeder lines to canals or rivers, into trunk lines that transported freight and passengers independent of steamboats. By 1860, 30,625 miles of track had been laid in the United States. By 1890, there were 167,191 miles of track in the country; and by the end of the century, 200,000.

The railroads were the single most important factor in economic expansion during the last half of the nineteenth century. They made possible the settlement of the West, the spurt in agriculture, the mass production of goods.

Americans at first were elated with the railroads. Farmers invested in rail stocks, and local communities gave railroads bounties to pass through their towns. From 1850 to 1871, the federal government plied rail companies with 137 million acres of land (three or four times the size of New York State). Two hundred and ninety-four towns, cities, and counties in New York gave the carriers $30 million to run tracks through their areas. According to the governor of Kansas, four-fifths of the municipal debt in his state was committed to help railroad construction. The land given to private rail owners included one-fourth of the states of Minnesota and Washington; one-fifth of Wisconsin, Iowa, Kansas, North Dakota, and Montana; and one-eighth of California.

It soon became obvious, however, that the railroad promoters were not as public-spirited as the farmers and city folk had hoped. They inflated construction costs, bribed legislators, watered stocks, and arranged fraudulent bankruptcies, passing the costs on to the public. The carriers squeezed small business people mercilessly, while helping rich allies become much richer. On one hand, they gave handsome rebates, for instance, to John D. Rockefeller and his Standard Oil Company, which made it possible for the oil tycoon to sell oil more cheaply and thus drive his competitors out of business. On the other hand, they hiked rates for small farmers. In the words of one fellow, the farmer farmed corn, but the railroads "farmed the farmers." In due course, the railroads became the most hated institution in the United States.

The railroad owners' attitude toward their workers was as callous as their attitude toward the public at large. Wages were relatively low—a brakeman in 1877 averaged $1.75 for a 12-hour day. And the work was extremely dangerous. In Massachusetts alone, forty-two railroad workers were killed through accidents in one year. And since there was no workmen's compensation, widows had to go to court to be compensated for their losses—if they were successful in proving the railroad negligent.

It was because of problems with accidents that twelve locomotive engineers met in Detroit in 1863 to form what later became the Brotherhood of Locomotive Engineers. Within the next decade, conductors and foremen followed suit. But these were not very militant unions; their concern was with matters other than wages and hours.

Even so, the carriers were harsh in dealing with them. Michigan Central's president ordered his superintendent to find out who the union leaders were and "let them go one at a time." The Baltimore & Ohio president, John W. Garrett, fired a committee of firemen who tried to make an appointment with him. Gowen of the Reading ordered his locomotive engineers to quit either their brotherhood or their jobs; when half of them went on strike, he gave raises to the "loyal" men and fired the others.

That was the tenor of things in the railroad industry when the best-known banking firm in the country, Jay Cooke & Company, went bankrupt in 1873. In the next three years, twenty-three thousand businesses followed suit. Within seven years, real wages were down by almost half. Out of a population of only 40 million, 3 million people were jobless. That would be like 17 million today.

"Never was a time . . . when a greater amount of misery, poverty, and wretchedness existed than at the present time," reported the Washington *Inter-Ocean*. Those workers who didn't lose their jobs were often forced to take wage cuts. Three thousand textile workers in Fall River, Massachusetts, went on strike against a second pay reduction during 1874. They won after a month on the picket line, but management soon tried to restore the reduction, again causing a stoppage throughout the city. This time, after eight weeks and a confrontation with the state militia, the union was totally defeated. The textile workers returned to the mills, signed "iron-clad oaths" that they would not join a union in the future, and watched helplessly as their leaders were discharged and blacklisted.

It was in this atmosphere that a minor railroad incident ballooned into what someone called two weeks of insurrection, causing the death of more than a hundred workers and serious injury for many more.

In March 1877, the heads of four trunk lines secretly met in New York. Among the decisions they made was to impose another wage cut on their employees and to insure themselves against possible strikes. If any of the four were hit with a work stoppage, the other three would pay its losses until the strike was over.

There was no urgent reason for this action. Quite a few smaller carriers had gone bankrupt during the depression, but the larger ones were in excellent condition. The New York Central had paid its usual 8 percent dividend throughout the depression and enjoyed earnings of almost twice that amount. The Pennsylvania, the largest railroad in the country, was also in good shape. But on May 24, Thomas A. Scott, its president, declared a second 10 percent reduction in pay. When a delegation of workers went to see him, the suave Scott convinced them that they ought to wait until the depression was over. Only a group of a hundred longshoremen who worked for the Pennsylvania on its docks in New York went on strike—their pay had been reduced from 20 cents an hour in 1873 to 13½ cents. They were fired and replaced with clerks. The strike collapsed.

A day after the second wage cut went into effect on the Pennsylvania, a group of workers on one of its subsidiaries met in a town near Pittsburgh and formed the Trainmen's Union. Unlike the Brotherhoods, which were based on crafts—engineers, firemen, conductors, each in a separate organization—the Trainmen's Union embraced all trades. It was an industrial union. Its leader, Robert A. Ammon, a powerfully built young man not yet twenty-five, was college educated and the son of an affluent insurance man. He secretly enrolled a few hundred members, but his activities were uncovered and he was discharged. Even so, he and forty associates made a last try to call a general strike for June 27. Unfortunately the leaders were divided on how long to wait and how to conduct the strike. Only a few hundred men responded to the call.

Two weeks later, however, a small incident on the Baltimore & Ohio, involving only forty men, flared into a labor war that engulfed the whole country. On July 11, the B & O, like other railroads, announced a second 10 percent wage cut. This was to go into effect July 16. On that afternoon, forty brakemen and firemen at Camden Junction near Baltimore decided they would not work. Some of these men had only recently joined the ill-fated Trainmen's Union. The strike, however, was not planned. It was spontaneous, a spur-of-the-moment action. The B & O had no trouble replacing the workers, but the strikers stopped another freight by convincing a fireman to quit his post. Forty policemen scattered the strikers. Seven freight trains left without incident, and everything seemed normal again.

In Martinsburg, West Virginia, however, the drama was repeated. Again twenty-five or thirty firemen left their jobs, and a large crowd of sympathizers gathered. The mayor had the strike leaders arrested, but the crowd, which included miners from nearby areas, released them. An attempt to start up the freight trains was frustrated. By morning, hundreds of other railroad workers had joined the strike, and the company dispatched a plea to Governor Henry M. Matthews to call out two companies of militia near Martinsburg. The militia appeared on the scene but refused to fight the strikers, many of whom were friends and relatives. Matthews himself led two more companies of militia, from Wheeling this time, but the hostility of the people along the way forced him to abandon the project.

"There is no disguising the fact that the strikers in all their lawful acts have the fullest sympathy of the community," reported the Baltimore *Sun*. "It is folly to blink at the fact that the manifestations of Public Opinion are almost everywhere in sympathy

Strikers against the Baltimore & Ohio Railroad drag firemen and engineers from a freight train in Martinsburg, West Virginia, in July 1877.

with the insurrection," said the New York *Tribune.* The strike spread to three other towns. Soon seventy trains with twelve hundred freight cars were being held up at Martinsburg.

At this point, the railroad corporation prevailed on the governor to ask President Rutherford B. Hayes for federal troops. Hayes responded immediately. A special train provided by the B & O delivered four hundred U.S. troops to the beleaguered city. When they arrived on the morning of July 19, they safely escorted two freight trains out of the city, and the next day thirteen more. Strike leaders were arrested, a request by the strikers for a compromise was haughtily rejected, and the B & O issued medals to workers who did not join the strike. It also promised them top priority in promotions. Everything seemed to be returning to normal.

On July 20, however, sixteen freights headed for Cumberland,

The National Guard firing on strikers and their sympathizers in Baltimore during the Baltimore & Ohio Railroad strike   LIBRARY OF CONGRESS

Maryland, ran into real trouble. Only one made it. Crowds of unemployed from the town's rolling mill, and many boys fourteen to eighteen, joined the railroaders to stop trains. When two strike leaders were arrested, swarms of people converged on the mayor's house and forced their release.

Before long, thousands of freight cars were standing still. Governor Lee Carroll of Maryland called out the National Guard, but he did not risk calling men from Cumberland; the strikers might be their friends. As the guardsmen sought to entrain in Baltimore, however, thousands of unemployed met them with a barrage of stones. A dozen were injured—but no one was killed as yet.

In the evening, some of the guardsmen, blocked from leaving their headquarters, began shooting indiscriminately. The strikers and their sympathizers refused to disperse, and before long there was a real shoot-out. An Irish tinner with no interest in the strike was shot in the stomach and died within two hours. An adolescent boy, shot in the groin, lay screaming on the sidewalk. A fifteen-year-old newsboy was killed, as were a shoemaker, a sixteen-year-old boy, and a man identified as an Arab. One soldier suffered a flesh wound.

By this time, fifteen thousand strike sympathizers had gathered around Camden Station, and someone set fire to the depot. The next day more crowds gathered. President Hayes sent troops to the scene from as far away as New York, on the theory that troops from the immediate vicinity would side with the demonstrators. At nightfall there was another confrontation with police and militiamen. Scores of people were wounded, many hundreds arrested, a lumberyard put on fire, a foundry attacked, and a train of oil cars set on fire. Thirteen people had been killed, dozens wounded.

The strike at this point was no longer confined to the B & O or Maryland and West Virginia. On July 18, firemen in Newark, Ohio, had stopped B & O freights, and brakemen and firemen detained passenger trains and freights of the Erie Railroad in Hornellsville, New York.

The big spillover, however, was on the Pennsylvania Railroad. On July 16, the company had announced that freights on its Pittsburgh division would be doubleheaders—two locomotives pulling twice as many cars as one did previously. The number of firemen and engineers would remain the same, but conductors and brakemen faced a 50 percent layoff. On Thursday, July 19, when the doubleheaders were to start operating, no one expected trouble. But a flagman named August Harris, reading of events in Martinsburg, announced he would not work. The rest of his crew joined him. Twenty-five other men were asked by the company to take their place but refused. They were fired on the spot. Three yardmen who volunteered were roughed up and forced to flee. Then as each new train came into the rail yard, its crew joined the walkout. Hundreds of workers from nearby factories, as well as unemployed people, joined a crowd at Twenty-eighth Street.

No trains ran that Thursday and Friday or for the next few days. Though the militia was called out by the governor's office, it was slow to mobilize; the men were so sympathetic to the strikers, they were in fact useless. The strikers continued to stop incoming trains, and the five hundred militiamen refused to intervene. Since the Pittsburgh militia was "untrustworthy," Governor John F. Hartranft now turned to troops from Philadelphia. At the behest of the Pennsylvania Railroad, the First Division of the state's National Guard was put on a Pennsylvania train at 2 A.M. The railroad's president was sure the guardsmen would put matters straight in Pittsburgh.

In due course the thousand guardsmen arrived, after being stoned in Harrisburg, Johnstown, and Altoona. They marched along the tracks, with seventeen deputy sheriffs in front of them, holding warrants for the arrest of eleven strikers. At one crossing they confronted a crowd estimated at between five thousand and twenty thousand. A few boys threw stones; a few men sitting on coal cars joined in a hail of coal.

The crowd was convinced the guardsmen would not shoot, but it was wrong. Without formal order, the muskets began firing two, three, four times a second. In less than five minutes, it was all over —twenty people lay dead; somewhere between thirty and seventy were badly injured, including fifteen militiamen, three children, and one woman. As the guardsmen ran off, the general in charge ordered them—belatedly—to stop shooting.

Now the real riot began. Thousands in Pittsburgh, including businessmen, doctors, and members of the Pittsburgh militia, seized the streets, determined "to fight the Pennsylvania Railroad" and to send "every damned Philadelphia soldier . . . home in a box." Bands of young people invaded gun shops and the armory. Men marched behind fife and drums as in real war. Every now and then, shots rang out on both sides.

Finally the crowd settled on a new weapon, fire. At 10:45 P.M., the first freight car was set afire and shoved down the grade. Coal cars and then oil cars were fed into the blaze—and firemen were prevented from dousing it, at pistol and cannon point. By midnight the fire could be seen many miles away. Men roamed the city, putting to fire whatever they could. A small cannon was taken from the Pittsburgh militia and aimed at the railroad's machine shop.

At this point, General Robert M. Brinton ordered his Philadelphia troops to fire. Before the cannon could get off its first shot, eleven more strikers were killed or wounded. The cannon never fired, but the rioters continued to put the torch to everything in sight—freight yards, the machine shop, freights filled with whiskey.

That day and the next, arson and looting replaced law and order in Pittsburgh. Hundreds of miners from nearby towns joined their railroad brethren; women brought sandwiches and coffee to the men at war. A grain elevator went up in smoke, as did twelve tenement houses, stables, a cooper's shop, and private homes.

As of Monday, July 23, 104 locomotives and 2,152 railroad cars lay in ashes, not to mention many buildings. An official coroner's report claimed twenty-four dead—undoubtedly a conservative figure. Scott estimated the property damage at $5 million—a lot of money in those days. That Monday and Tuesday, the police were out of sight. The city was patrolled by strikers and sympathizers. No freight trains moved in or out.

Governor Hartranft mobilized ten thousand guardsmen, and President Hayes sent in three thousand federal troops to deal with the existing chaos. Violence would not abate, however. In Reading, six workers were killed, and more would have died if one regiment of guardsmen had not threatened to shoot another unless the harassment of strikers ceased. The president met with his cabinet every day to map military strategy, and troops and ships were deployed to guard the city itself. On July 25, when almost all the rail lines in the central and western states were caught up in the freight blockade, President Hayes threatened to impose martial law throughout the country.

A week after the strike had begun, the United States had the appearance of a nation near revolution. Newspapers were comparing the situation in Pittsburgh with the Paris commune and seizure of the city of Paris by Marxist radicals in 1871. The New York *World* reported that Pittsburgh was "in the hands of men dominated by the devilish spirit of communism."

The strike that began on the B & O lines soon involved the Pennsylvania, the Erie, the New York Central, and moved westward until it finally included the Central Pacific on the West Coast. All of this happened spontaneously—the railroad men had no union or national leadership to guide them. But quite soon the Workingmen's party, a socialist party that believed in the principles of Karl Marx, began organizing meetings in support of the strike, in Cincinnati, Boston, Philadelphia, New York, San Francisco, Paterson, Brooklyn, Newark. The socialists called for an 8-hour day, abolition of conspiracy laws against unions, and goverment ownership of all railroads and telegraph lines. Their message made an impact. In Cincinnati and other cities where small delegations of leftists visited the rail yards, they induced the workers to join the national strike.

In Chicago and Saint Louis, the Marxists had their greatest impact. Only six years before, Chicago had been devastated by a great fire, but it was rebuilding rapidly. Among its half million population, 15 percent were German Americans, large numbers of them belonging to the Workingmen's party.

As news of the rail strike filled the front pages of the Chicago press—including a pro-labor penny sheet, the *Daily News*—socialists held meetings to gain support for it. Albert Parsons, an American-born socialist who was a leader of the party, led the way with one ringing speech after another.

On Monday, July 23, while the strike was gaining momentum in the East, forty switchmen on the Michigan Central had walked off the job. Before sundown the next day, the leftists and their friends—the Chicago *Tribune* called them "an uncombed, unwashed mob of guttersnipes and loafers"—were appealing not only to railroad workers but to workers in the stockyards, factories, stores, and docks to join the strike. Wherever they went, the mob was chased and clubbed by police, but the wave became a tidal wave.

Parsons and his comrades tried to contain the violence, but workers who had been abused by the police could not be restrained. On Wednesday and Thursday, July 25 and 26, the strike flared into warfare. Lumbermen, tailors, sailors, longshoremen, and factory workers left their jobs and took to the streets. Saloons were closed; the streetcars stopped running on the South Side.

City authorities gave guns to thousands of men to defend the city from the "communists." General Philip H. Sheridan, who was fighting Indians in Sioux country, was ordered to return to Chicago at once. All day Wednesday, fifty groups of strikers chased militiamen and the volunteer special police. A thousand leftists shouted at scabs and fought police on a road leading to the McCormick Reaper Works. Locomotives were destroyed at the Burlington roundhouse on West Sixteenth Street.

By now the city was being patrolled by at least ten thousand regular officers, special police, and troops. On Thursday morning, a battle ensued between city forces and ten thousand strikers at the Halsted Street Viaduct. When it was over, a dozen men and women on labor's side lay dead; a hundred were arrested. Scuffles, small and large, occurred in scores of places. In two days, somewhere between thirty and fifty people had been killed; many more were wounded. The mob's anger, however, had burned itself out. On Saturday the first freight left Chicago under military escort.

The strike hit another peak of sorts in Saint Louis, where the socialist movement seized the government. The Workingmen's party in Saint Louis numbered about a thousand members, two-thirds of them German-speaking. On July 22, it had held a mass meeting condemning "the government for its action in sending

Police and soldiers charging strikers at the Halsted Street Viaduct in ▶ Chicago, July 26, 1877   LIBRARY OF CONGRESS

FRANK LESLIE'S ILLUSTRATED NEWSPAPER

Entered according to the Act of Congress, in the year 1877, by FRANK LESLIE, in the Office of the Librarian of Congress at Washington.

No. 1,141—Vol. XLIV.]

NEW YORK, AUGUST 11, 1877.

[PRICE, 10 CENTS.

troops to protect capitalists and their property against the just demands of railway men."

That afternoon the party sent five hundred people across the Mississippi River to East Saint Louis, where they were greeted by a thousand railroaders and friends who immediately joined the strike. Back on the other side of the river, the party succeeded in shutting down not only the Missouri Pacific and other rails but many businesses and factories.

Laclede Gas Works became so alarmed, it canceled a 25 percent wage cut that had gone into effect July 1. Missouri Pacific offered to restore recently cut wages to their old levels.

By July 29, the city was paralyzed. President Hayes sent in troops, and merchants raised $15,000 to arm one thousand "specials." The Workingmen's party was unable to withstand such pressure. To add to its woes, police raided its headquarters and arrested seventy-three of its leaders. Four were eventually sentenced to five years in jail and fined $3000 each.

After Saint Louis, the strike sputtered for a couple of days, but the two-week insurrection had now spent itself. A simple stoppage by forty railroaders to protest a wage cut had escalated beyond what anyone could have foreseen. The combined power of the corporations and the federal goverment had broken the strike and set back the union movement in the United States for years.

The Debs Revolution

I can hire one-half of the working class
to kill the other half.

Jay Gould

At the time of the Civil War, the nation ranked fourth among industrial nations. By 1894 it was first, eclipsing all rivals in the manufacture of commodities. It was now producing twice as much as Britain, the previous world leader. The boom was so strong that 5½ million immigrants were attracted to the United States in just ten years. The number of factory workers doubled from less than 3 million to almost 6 million. Railroad mileage, too, almost doubled; the United States had more track than did all of Europe.

Yet, there was a widening inequality. President Grover Cleveland observed that big trusts were growing, but workers were "far in the rear," being "trampled to death beneath an iron heel." "There are too many millionaires and too many paupers," cried the Hartford *Courant.* The United States Census Bureau indicated a decline in average income of 20 to 25 percent.

Corporation officials remained bitterly hostile to unions and union people. "Give the workingmen and strikers gun-bullet food for a few days," was the advice of Thomas A. Scott, president of the Pennsylvania Railroad. It was advice that did not go unheeded. A New York *Sun* article in September 1886 described a police attack against ten thousand people during a streetcar strike, in which "men with broken scalps were crawling off in all directions and squabbling children were knocked every way by their daddies who were flying from the clubs." Hundreds of strikers were arrested, many charged with that ancient crime, conspiracy.

Typical of the harsh confrontation between labor and capital was the 1892 strike of 3,800 steelworkers at Homestead, Pennsylvania. The mills there—owned by Andrew Carnegie, a Scotsman who was to become known as a great philanthropist—were quite profitable. There was no need to cut wages; but on the expiration of a three-year contract, Carnegie's associate, Henry Clay Frick, advised 800 skilled workers that their wages would be cut 18 to 26 percent and the company would no longer deal with their union.

A strike ensued. The 3,000 unskilled men joined their skilled brethren—and in time-honored fashion, Frick hired the Pinkerton Detective Agency to bring in strikebreakers from New York, Philadelphia, and Chicago. Three hundred blacklegs were put on barges below Pittsburgh and sent silently up the river to Homestead.

As the Pinkertons sought to embark, shots rang out. The battle lasted from early morning to five in the afternoon. The climax came when strikers mounted a small brass cannon and set fire to barrels of oil that they had poured on the water near the barges. Under this assault, the Pinkertons ran up the white flag of surrender, as if in actual war. Nine strikers and three Pinkertons lay dead. Shortly after five o'clock, the strikebreakers were marched to the skating rink of this town of 12,000, taunted and attacked by strikers' wives along the way.

The victory, however, was short-lived. On July 10, the governor of Pennsylvania mobilized 8,000 National Guardsmen to patrol

Troops entering Homestead, Pennsylvania, July 1892   LIBRARY OF
CONGRESS

the Homestead plant and two others that had joined the strike. Carnegie and Frick sent out seventy recruiting agents to hire strikebreakers; the guardsmen escorted them into the premises and protected them in their bunkhouses.

What the Pinkertons and guardsmen started, the courts completed. On July 18, 1892, seven strike leaders were indicted for the murder of a Pinkerton; two months later, a grand jury handed down 167 true bills—indictments—charging various leaders with murder, conspiracy, and aggravated riot. The strikers had been receiving about $10,000 a week to feed their members, but by November they could hold out no longer. They voted by a narrow margin to try and get their jobs back; the strike was broken.

Homestead was still in the headlines when an equally violent strike broke out in the silver and lead mines of the Coeur d'Alene district of Idaho. The miners had been successful in two previous strikes in forcing the mineowners to restore wage cuts. But this year they were attacked by National Guardsmen, and they fell in defeat. Six hundred of them were placed in "bull pens"—outdoor jails, in effect—at Kellogg and Wallace. Fifteen were eventually sentenced to jail. There were other strikes—of railroad workers in

Striking steelworkers in Homestead, Pennsylvania, watch for scabs arriving by train.   LIBRARY OF CONGRESS

Buffalo, for instance—that were equally militant and equally unsuccessful.

In 1893 the nation was hit by still another depression. On May 4, the National Cordage Company, which had paid an unbelievable 100 percent dividend only five months before, went bankrupt.

In "Pottersville," a village of shacks built to house strikebreakers in Homestead, Pennsylvania   LIBRARY OF CONGRESS

Sixteen thousand other bankruptcies followed. Thousands of factories closed, more than a tenth of the railroad mileage in the country was placed in receivership, and 3 million workers found themselves jobless and hungry.

In the midst of the depression, George M. Pullman, the highly successful manufacturer of the sleeping cars and dining cars attached to trains, decided to cut the wages of his six thousand employees. The round-faced Pullman, with high forehead, intense brown eyes, brown hair, and small chin-beard, lived in a $350,000 mansion on Chicago's fashionable Prairie Avenue and traveled in a specially constructed $38,000 railroad car—both fabulous sums at the time. Pullman had built what he called a model town, just south of Chicago (now part of the city), to house his factories and his workers. His publicists called it "a new idea"; labor leader George Schilling called it "a slave pen without an equal."

The community was situated on a four-thousand-acre site, and seemed most attractive—from a distance. Its streets were wide and clean; its neat brick houses were arranged around a square landscaped with lawns and flowers. In its large arcade were housed a post office, stores, an opera house, a library, a kindergarten, and a YMCA. Beyond were retail stores and blocks of three-story brick tenements.

Fifty-five hundred workers lived in Pullman's tenements, worked in his shops, prayed at churches rented from him, sent their children to schools built by him, relaxed in his park, and as one worker put it, were "buried in the Pullman cemetery and went to the Pullman hell." Even the gas and waterworks belonged to the company.

Since its formation in 1867, the Pullman company had always paid at least an 8 percent dividend. The value of its shares had gone up from about $100,000 to $36 million, and the firm had $25 million in surpluses that would be distributed as a stock dividend four years later. In 1892 and 1893, business was so good that profits were almost equal to the full amount the company paid out in wages.

But in the summer of 1893, Pullman executed a double squeeze. He laid off almost half his work force and cut the wages of the remaining 3,100 by 28 percent. In December, steamfitters and blacksmiths went on strike, but without success. Then in March and April 1894, the men started forming branches of the new American Railway Union (ARU) and soon had 4,000 members.

A committee of forty-six men was chosen to discuss the wage cuts with Pullman; but, though the sleeping-car magnate was polite, he refused to budge. The next day, three of the committee members were laid off—despite a pledge by Pullman that there would be no such reprisal—and their fellow workers went on strike.

From this relatively minor incident, a national conflict ensued. For a month the strike remained a local affair, completely peaceful. It was also completely ineffective, because the sleeping cars were still being attached to all trains, and the suspension of new palace-car production was only a minor irritant for Pullman. The company refused to arbitrate the dispute. There was "nothing to arbitrate," said the vice president.

But on June 12, 1894, things changed. Four hundred railroaders from across the country were meeting that day at Uhlich's Hall in Chicago, at the first national convention of the American Railway Union.

The American Railway Union was the brainchild of the most beloved union leader of the nineteenth century, Eugene V. Debs. He was one of ten children born to French Alsatian parents in Terre Haute, Indiana. Debs' first job, at fourteen, was scraping grease from freight trains of the Vandalia Railroad for 50 cents a day. A year and a half later, he was promoted to locomotive fireman at $1 a night. He worked at the craft for a few years, but when a friend slipped under a locomotive and was killed, Debs' mother prevailed on him to quit the railroad and get a job with a wholesale grocery.

In his free time, however, Debs visisted friends at the rail yards and remained a member of the Brotherhood of Locomotive Firemen (BLF). A talented and well-liked young man, he soon was chosen secretary of the local union branch, then moved up steadily until he became the Brotherhood's national secretary-treasurer and editor of its newspaper. Debs worked a full year without pay and rebuilt the BLF so that by 1883 it had 8,000 members.

There was nothing particularly radical about Debs at the time. He had refused to support the 1877 rail strike because he believed that labor disputes should be resolved by "reason and compromise." Instead of strikes, he urged arbitration by an outside arbitrator. Ultimately he would become a socialist and the presidential candidate of the Socialist party five times; but in the 1870s and 1880s, he was still a member of the Democratic party. He was elected city clerk of Terre Haute in 1879 and a member of the state legislature five years later, both on the Democratic party ticket.

But Debs began to nurture doubts about craft unions—unions of a single craft. His own BLF had grown under his stewardship from 2,000 to 20,000 members; yet only 10 percent of the 900,000 workers in the railroad industry belonged to unions, and they seemed to be making little progress. By pitting one craft against another, the carriers were able to defeat them all.

An example of this was a strike on the Burlington line in 1888. When the company threatened to seek injunctions against the Brotherhood leaders, P. M. Arthur of the engineers' union broke ranks and ordered his members back to work. The strike collapsed. Four years later, other railway crafts refused to help Buffalo switchmen in a similar situation. Debs decided, therefore, to form an industrial union of railroad workers. "Justice to labor will never come in my judgment," he told the press, "until labor federates and wields its united power for the good of all."

The American Railway Union—composed of all crafts in a single organization—was established in June 1893 and was an instant success. When it was just a few months old, it conducted a successful eighteen-day strike against James J. Hill's Great Northern Railroad, a carrier with twenty-five hundred miles of track and 9,000 employees. The company was forced to restore almost the entire amount of three wage cuts—$16 a month. The voice of labor was bound to be heard, said the Salt Lake *Tribune,* when "a corporation of so gigantic proportions had to yield so quickly to their men." The ARU recruited new members, sometimes at the rate of 2,000 a day. Within a year it had 150,000 members, not much smaller than the AFL at that time, and considerably larger than all the old railroad Brotherhoods combined.

It was to this ARU, at its first regular convention in 1894, that the striking Pullman workers came with their problem. They asked the ARU to boycott all Pullman cars: to refuse to operate trains that had a Pullman sleeping car attached to it.

Sitting in the president's chair, Debs was torn between logic and emotion. He sympathized fully with the strikers, of course—his attitude toward strikes had made a 180-degree turn. But he was aware of recent defeats suffered by labor. Jacob Coxey's army of 10,000 unemployed had marched on Washington demanding re-

Eugene V. Debs, who led the American Railway Union

lief but had come back with empty hands. An eight-week strike of 180,000 mine workers had ended with the usual setback.

To take on Pullman meant dealing not only with the palace-car king but with the General Managers' Association (GMA). It represented twenty-four carriers who owned forty-one thousand miles of track and employed 221,000 workers. Nonetheless, Debs decided to help the Pullman strikers. The convention voted to cease operations at two Pullman plants, in Ludlow, Kentucky, and Saint Louis, and to institute a national boycott against all sleepers.

The boycott began slowly on June 26. At the Twelfth Street station of the Illinois Central in Chicago, the *Diamond Special* took off for St. Louis with the sleeping car still coupled to it. But the next shift of switchmen refused to handle sleepers, and the day crew did likewise. As expected, management fired those who would not switch Pullman cars—and fellow workers in turn walked off the job in sympathy. Within a day, 3,500 Illinois Central employees were out of work, and the boycott-strike had spread to fourteen other lines. Ultimately, 260,000 workers went on strike. *The New York Times* called it "the greatest battle between labor and capital that has ever been inaugurated in the United States."

Had it just been a conflict between labor and capital, the American Railway Union very likely would have won. "The country had never before seen a strike so well organized and on so large a scale," wrote historian Samuel Yellen. Of the twenty-four railroads fanning out of Chicago, thirteen were entirely stalled and the other eleven were running little more than mail and passenger cars.

The General Managers' Association, acting for the twenty-four railroads emanating out of Chicago, tried to hire strikebreakers from near and far, including 2,000 from Canada. But they were not very successful. It wasn't because of threats by strikers. On the contrary, Debs repeatedly urged against the use of violence. A government commission later reported that "there is no evidence before the commission that the officers of the American Railway

Union at any time participated in or advised intimidation, violence, or destruction of property." It wasn't necessary. The union had great support from the public—tens of thousands of people wore white armbands, the ARU emblem. "You cannot go a block," wrote an AFL organizer, "without you see some people wearing a white ribbon." Railroad workers throughout the nation responded to the ARU call.

The Pullman Company, however, had the support of the influential General Managers' Association, and the GMA had the support of the federal government. The government eventually broke the strike.

Between them, the GMA and the federal government created a climate of hysteria that made it possible to use violence against the strikers on an unprecedented scale. Among the sensational headlines of the day were:

ANARCHISTS ON WAY TO AMERICA FROM EUROPE

FROM A STRIKE TO A REVOLUTION

ANARCHISTS AND SOCIALISTS SAID TO BE PLANNING
THE DESTRUCTION AND LOOTING OF THE TREASURY

The GMA opened offices in a half dozen cities to recruit strikebreakers, and the federal government, through injunctions and force, made it possible for those strikebreakers to function. The result was violence during which many people were killed and injured and mountains of property destroyed.

The president of the United States in 1894 was Grover Cleveland, a Democrat. His attorney general, Richard B. Olney, was a man with strong ties to the railroad corporations. Prior to taking the government job, he had been a corporation lawyer specializing in railroad affairs for thirty-five years. He owned a considerable amount of stock in the railroads and had been a director of a number of lines, including the strike-bound Burlington and the Boston & Maine, of which George Pullman was a codirector. He had also been a member of the General Managers' Association, the very organization that was directly pitted against the strikers.

When the boycott of Pullman cars began, Olney promised to use "overwhelming" force against the strikers and ordered federal marshals to hire special deputies to protect the mail cars usually attached to trains. Thousands were recruited, five thousand in Chicago alone. Significantly, most of those deputies were appointed by the railroad companies, though they were paid by the government. There is considerable dispute as to whether any deputies at all were needed to defend the mail cars. Eugene Debs had publicly offered to assign union crews to operate any train with a mail car, providing it did not also have a sleeper on it.

On June 30, with the strike only a few days old, Edwin Walker, a railroad attorney who had recently represented the GMA, was appointed by Olney as special counsel for the federal government in Chicago. Walker's job was to assist railroads in securing injunctions against the strikers—injunctions that would be enforced by federal troops and the special deputies. On July 2, Walker applied for a federal court injunction. He argued that the strike violated the Sherman Antitrust Act—a law originally passed to curb business monopolies but now being used against unions. Without hearing a single union witness, federal judges Peter S. Grosscup and William A. Woods granted the most sweeping injunction against strikers in American history. It forbade strike leaders from taking any action on behalf of the strike—even communicating with a striker, or sending telegrams or answering questions about the injunction. Under the injunction, it was illegal to "persuade a railroad worker to join the strike or stay on strike," even if the persuasion was peaceful. "It is seriously questioned," wrote the U.S. Strike Commission later, "whether courts have jurisdiction to enjoin citizens from 'persuading' each other in industrial or other matters of common interest."

Nonetheless, the federal injunction and the state injunctions modeled on it had their impact. A rail worker in Albuquerque was sentenced to fifteen days in jail for refusing to get on an engine and fire it. Others were arrested for refusing to turn on switches.

U. S. Infantry with a patrolling train at Blue Island, Illinois, during the 1894 railroad strike   LIBRARY OF CONGRESS

On July 3, Walker, Judge Grosscup, and others sent telegrams to Washington asking that troops be sent to Chicago to enforce the injunction. There had been some violence in Blue Island, a suburb of Chicago, but it had petered out. Those who signed the telegram said an immediate general strike was about to take place, but in fact things were still fairly quiet.

However, Cleveland did sent troops to the Windy City—over the objection, incidentally, of his secretary of war, Daniel S. Lamont. The president's action, some writers say, may have been illegal because the Constitution provides that in such cases the president must have the approval of the state governor and state legislature. In Illinois, both were opposed to Cleveland's dispatch of troops. So were the governors of Kansas, Colorado, Texas, and Oregon. The militia had been called out in twenty states and seemed able to handle matters adequately without federal troops.

Governor Altgeld of Illinois sent an angry telegram to President Cleveland, saying that his action was unnecessary. "Our railroads," he said, "are paralyzed not by reason of obstruction, but because they cannot get men to operate their trains."

The show of force by the authorities created a tense climate. On July 4 in Chicago, some people congregated on railroad tracks, turned over a few freight cars, and set them ablaze. The next day the situation grew worse. Ten thousand people marched eastward on Rock Island property, again setting fire to freights and throwing switches.

The troops did not use firearms, but they did attack the crowd with drawn bayonets and injure some people.

The crowd, however, could not be dispersed, nor the railroad cars moved. When two hundred soldiers and three hundred deputy marshals tried to take out a trainload of livestock at the Union Stock Yards, they were halted by strikers a mile away and had to abandon the effort after four hours. The next day, a large fire was set at the World's Columbian Exposition in Jackson Park; it consumed seven buildings and sent a pall of smoke that could be seen miles away.

That evening, at the request of Chicago's mayor, Governor Peter Altgeld sent five militia regiments to Chicago. The tempo of opposition was growing. Unfortunately, few people seemed to notice that Debs had offered that day to call off the strike immediately if Pullman would agree to arbitrate. This offer too was disregarded.

Property losses up to that point were still small. But on July 6, they multiplied—$340,000 worth of railroad property was burned or otherwise destroyed. Six thousand strikers and sympathizers roamed the streets. Not far from the town of Pullman, a deputy killed an innocent bystander.

Violence was in the air. Sure enough, on July 7, Illinois National

Guardsmen fired into a mob after four guardsmen had been injured. At least four civilians were killed (some said twenty or thirty) and twenty wounded, including a few women. There were similar conflicts in Denver, San Francisco, and elsewhere. On July 9, President Cleveland issued an order prohibiting any kind of meetings in Illinois. The next day he extended the order to six other states, including California.

While this drama was going on in Chicago, similar ones were taking place in other areas. In Trinidad, Colorado, on July 1, strikers and their friends disarmed forty-eight deputy sheriffs. The next day, the president sent five companies of U.S. troops to the scene. They arrested forty-eight ringleaders. At Raton, New Mexico, the county sheriff refused to act against the five hundred ARU members on strike. When a U.S. marshal and eighty-five federal troops entered the town, hotel workers joined the strike. In a small mining town three miles away, a crowd shoved sixteen cars down the grade to block tracks at Raton.

In Los Angeles, five militia companies expressed sympathy for the strikers and refused to act against them. The federal government finally broke the strike in that city by placing troops on every train. At Sacramento, after many state militiamen refused to move against the strikers, 542 federal troops were landed by ship. They attacked the unionists with fixed bayonets. In a dozen other places, similar scenes were being enacted—in Oakland, California; in Wyoming, Nebraska, Utah, Nevada, Montana. The number of casualties is not known exactly, but a general estimate was that twenty-five strikers were killed and sixty seriously injured. Seven hundred and five strikers were jailed.

The behavior of the government stirred sympathy for the Pullman strike both within the labor movement and with the general public. Within the American Federation of Labor, a ground swell began to build for a nationwide strike of all unionized workers in the country. And in Chicago on July 8, representatives of a hundred unions agreed to call a citywide strike if the national rail stoppage was not settled by 4 P.M. July 10.

It was already too late, however. That day two more people were killed by troops in Spring Valley, Illinois. That day, too, Eugene Debs and three associates were arrested on charges of criminal conspiracy. While they were in jail awaiting bond of $10,000 each, to be put up by two friendly saloonkeepers, the deputy marshals raided ARU headquarters and ransacked the office so thoroughly that it had to be abandoned. The union had no place in which to work or to receive messages and telegrams from its affiliates.

The general strike in Chicago petered out on July 11, when only twenty-five thousand responded to the call. By then it was obvious that the federal troops were clearing the tracks and would soon restore operations. The AFL leadership, meeting the next day, concluded that "a general strike at this time is inexpedient." Debs was treated courteously and given $1,000 for the strike, but nothing more.

The strike clearly was beaten. Debs offered to end it on the single condition that all strikers be allowed to return to their jobs, but the General Managers' Association did not even reply.

On July 17, the four ARU leaders were re-arrested, on the charge of contempt of court for violating the injunction. The bail again was $10,000 each, but this time Debs and his associates decided to remain in jail. Two days later, twenty-three new indictments were handed down, charging the same four as well as seventy-one others with violating a host of federal statutes. In the same week, tonnage on the ten trunk lines moving eastward went up by 700 percent; it was now two-thirds of prestrike levels.

Meanwhile George Pullman posted notices in his town, stating that his shops would be reopened. Only 325 workers responded to his call to return to work; but by August 1, enough were available to put the plants back in operation.

The defeat of the strike was a death blow to the ARU. On August 2, it held a special convention, with only fifty-two delegates present. Three days later it called off the strike.

The epilogue to the Debs Rebellion was written in the courts.

Debs was sentenced to six months in jail, his three associates to three months each. It was not until February 1895 that the conspiracy charge came up in Judge Grosscup's court. Clarence Darrow, the former railroad attorney who now represented the union, announced that he would call Pullman and members of the General Managers' Association to the stand to prove that it was they, not the union, that had engaged in conspiracy. Pullman slipped out of town to avoid testifying. GMA members said they couldn't remember what happened. Darrow demanded that the GMA produce minutes of its meetings, but at this point a juror became ill and Judge Grosscup adjourned the trial. It never reconvened.

Racketeers

Racketeering is . . . the introduction of foreign
bodies into the content of unionism.
                              Professor Jack Barbash,
                              University of Wisconsin

The nineteenth-century leaders of the labor movement by and large were dedicated and idealistic people.

"I love this union cause," said William H. Sylvis, head of the National Labor Union after the Civil War. "I hold it more dear than I do my family or my life. I am willing to devote to it all that I am or have or hope for in this world." Though he was the leader of the most important union of his time, he never had enough money to pay his bills. His clothes were usually worn down to bare thread, and he and his wife and five children frequently experienced hunger. When he died prematurely at the age of forty-one, there was not enough money in the house to bury him.

There were innumerable people in the labor movement who had the same ideals as Sylvis, who loved "this union cause." But by the beginning of the twentieth century, there were some union leaders who looked upon unions as a business, a chance to make money for themselves. Most of these business unionists won wage increases and other benefits for their members. They were not dishonest, not crooks, just people who considered themselves practical rather than idealistic. A few, however, *were* crooks—extortionists who gave the labor movement a bad name. They called strikes and broke strikes, not to further the cause of labor but primarily to benefit themselves.

How did these racketeers get into the union movement? It's a complicated story.

In the last third of the nineteenth century, the American economy was prospering—growing far more rapidly than that of England or Germany. This period, therefore, was a time of transition, both for the nation and the labor movement. In certain industries, such as steel, the battle between labor and capital remained fierce. Unions were unable to gain a foothold. In others, such as construction, there was a violent conflict to begin with; but unions won a fair share of strikes, and in due course the employers accepted them as a fact of life. These unions became strong and stable.

Perhaps because of this, union leaders had two different approaches to the purpose of their organizations. Some radicals, like the feisty socialist Daniel De Leon, argued that the main purpose of unions was not to win wage increases but to overthrow the capitalist system itself. Others—most of them also radicals, like Samuel Gompers, a cigar maker, and Peter J. McGuire, a carpenter—believed that unions should concentrate on immediate objectives such as shorter hours and higher wages. The overthrow of capitalism should be left to socialist parties.

Gompers and McGuire became the architects of a new kind of unionism, one that existed only in the United States—simple unionism. They, like De Leon, believed in socialism in principle. But they also felt that unions should concentrate their efforts on practical goals. Gompers described this philosophy in a single word: *more*—more wages, more leisure, more social benefits.

Simple unionists stated, "We have no ultimate demands. We are

Samuel Gompers, founder of the American Federation of Labor
LIBRARY OF CONGRESS

going on from day to day. We fight only for immediate objects—objects that can be realized in a few years." They believed that unionists should use the strike weapon to win more bread and butter, not to establish a labor party or work for government ownership of industry.

Gompers had an immense effect on the American labor movement. Born in 1850 in England, of Dutch Jewish parents, he came to the United States and went to work as a cigar maker. Most cigar makers were foreign-born and many belonged to Karl Marx's International Workingmen's Association. At age twenty-five,

Gompers became president of a New York local union of cigar makers. And at age thirty-six, he and forty-one other union leaders came together in Columbus, Ohio, to form the American Federation of Labor.

The AFL was an astounding success. It eventually grew to 10 million members. It was the first federation of labor to survive a depression; all others had gone out of business during economic slumps. The practical AFL, however, was able to ride out the storms.

Beginning in 1890, at least three out of five unionists were AFL members. The dramatic victory by AFL carpenters in gaining an 8-hour day, as well as gains made by AFL coal miners, attracted large numbers of skilled craftsmen to simple unionism. Until the CIO was organized in 1935, never more than 10 percent of all workers belonged to unions; but of those, the largest number were skilled craftsmen in the AFL.

If simple unionism was a success, however, it also had its problems. Men like Gompers and McGuire were honest and dedicated. But gradually the AFL was penetrated by others who considered the unions a business like other businesses. On the fringe of these business unionists were the racketeers, a small group of hustlers and criminals who used the labor movement much like the gangsters in Al Capone's day used the liquor industry—to make a fast buck by any means possible.

Perhaps the best way to illustrate how racketeering began and what its purpose was is to begin with the walking delegate.

In 1883, according to labor legend, a New York carpenter named James Lynch became the first union walking delegate. Union affairs hitherto had been handled by a job steward in his spare time, before and after work. Lynch was taken off the job and paid by his fellow workers to walk from place to place, enforcing apprentice rules, collecting dues, organizing new workers, and handling other tasks.

The hiring of Lynch was a response to practical problems. One of them was that fly-by-night subcontractors were using nonunion men to install doors, stairs, or windows in half-finished buildings. Before the job stewards knew what was going on, the windows or doors were installed and the nonunion men had vanished. The walking delegate could oversee those projects more efficiently.

By 1890 there were walking delegates handling carpenters' union affairs in 100 cities. Other unions were following suit, particularly after employers began to blacklist active unionists following the Chicago Haymarket riot of 1886. Unionists were being fired simply for discussing a grievance. The walking delegate— soon to be called business agent—seemed like the solution to that problem too.

The first walking delegates were sincere men, workers at heart, responsive to members' wants. But in time many business agents became lords and masters of their unions.

This wasn't too difficult, because the skilled men had made many gains and were relatively satisfied. A study by Professor Thomas Sewall Adams of the University of Wisconsin early in the twentieth century showed that one of every two strikes called by unions ended in total victory; and if you included partially successful strikes, the victory ratio was two out of three. Unions of skilled workers were able to win concessions that were impossible in other countries. "Between 1866 and 1903," wrote Professor Adams, "real wages rose more than 100 percent in industry and more than 70 percent in agriculture." The workday, which had been 14 hours in 1840, fell to 10 hours, and for building trades workers to 8 hours.

Under those circumstances, many rank-and-file workers were willing to let their business agents run things, and the business agents often dominated union affairs. They abolished many rights previously enjoyed by members and made decisions themselves— for instance, the right to call a strike or call one off. Business agents were handling matters previously voted on by workers, and assumed the right to place members on jobs. With such power, a business agent could put his own supporters on the best jobs and those of his rivals on less desirable jobs. Given this power, it was

THE LABOR DESPOT.

THE supreme tyrant of the labor organizations is the walking delegate, the well-fed, well-paid official who performs the functions of a general overseer, and whose fiat is expected to be obeyed without protest or murmur. Not a few of the disastrous strikes of recent years were prolonged, if they were not instigated, by these representatives of the worst elements of discontent. Happily American workingmen seem now to be losing their respect for this class of petty despots, and it is hardly probable that they will be able in future to exercise any such autocratic power as they have so injuriously employed in the past.

It was the peculiarity of the recent great strike in London that it was spontaneous, that it was based upon a real grievance, was entirely free from coercive excesses on the part of would-be bosses, and that it had, from first to last, the genuine sympathy of the great body of the people. The sole obstacle to a settlement was the obstinacy of the dock companies, upon whom the demand for slightly increased compensation was made by the striking laborers. Against these stubborn dock directors were arrayed the merchants, the ship-owners, and all the high officials in church and state, such men as Cardinal Manning, the Lord Mayor, the Bishop of London, and Sir John Lubbock interfering actively in behalf of the strikers, while Lord Randolph Churchill and other men in official life ably championed their cause in public addresses. It was inevitable that, thus sustained, the men on strike should ultimately gain a substantial victory. It will be well if American workingmen shall learn the lesson that, with a just cause, and sustaining from all disorderly and offensive methods, they, too, can depend upon public sympathy, and will be much more likely to win their way than when pursuing an opposite course.

The caption on this wood engraving from an 1889 issue of *Frank Leslie's Illustrated Newspaper* attacks the walking delegate, whom it calls "the supreme tyrant of the labor organizations." LIBRARY OF CONGRESS

no trick at all for the business agent to run the union almost as if it were his own personal property. Instead of officials working *for* the union, many walking delegates became bosses *over* the union. They made all the vital decisions.

This didn't happen all at once or without resistance. The carpenters' union is an example. At the head of it from 1886 to 1900 was socialist Peter McGuire, who had built the organization from the ground up. The rank and file worshiped his integrity and spellbinding oratory.

Opposed to McGuire, however, were the new men of power, the business agents. Their first effort was to seek control of the executive board, then still made up of men who worked daily in the trade.

In 1890, because of McGuire's resistance, the business agents failed. They persevered but were again defeated by McGuire in 1892. However, they won a victory in 1894 when they placed in the hands of the union president—rather than the rank and file— the right to call strikes and call them off.

McGuire reversed all this in 1896 when he had the issue put to a national referendum of union members. It took the professional business agents another fifteen years before they finally achieved their goals. At the turn of the century, McGuire became a hopeless drunk. In 1902 he was forced to resign because of charges of embezzlement.

The man who replaced him, William Huber, had a different view of unions entirely. Huber condemned the socialists as "visionary, their schemes and isms . . . only the mouthings of irresponsible, imaginative fantastical doctrines." At the local levels, the business agents were entrenching themselves further, and some of them were becoming outright extortionists. Though Huber quit in 1915, the machine he built found itself in the firm hands of William L. Hutcheson, who ruled the carpenters' union until 1952. When he retired, he was so dominant in union affairs that he could turn over his job to his son, Maurice A. Hutcheson, with no overt opposition.

Some of the business agents went beyond being bureaucrats. They engaged in actions that were clearly illegal. They used their power to call strikes or not call them, in order to solicit bribes. A few examples illustrate how this worked.

The first well known labor racketeer was Sam Parks, head of Housesmith's Local 2 in New York. Parks was an ally of a large construction company. He helped that company earn big profits by never calling a strike against it. On the other hand, he called frequent strikes against its competitors, causing them long and costly delays.

Anyone who wanted a bridge built got the message. If he used Parks' favored company, the bridge got built without strikes and was finished on time. Otherwise it might be delayed by work stoppages called at Parks' whim for no reason except to help his corporate ally.

Parks did not wait for housesmiths to join his union through persuasion and discussion. If they hesitated, he slugged them into the union. In two months at the outset of his career, early in the twentieth century, ninety beatings were reported. Wages of the union men rose from $2.50 to $4.50 a day, but they lost thousands of dollars through phony strikes.

On one occasion Parks called out twelve hundred men of the Hecla Ironworks simply because the company refused to pay him a bribe. From 1901 through 1903, all of the building trades unions in New York fell into his powerful hands. On a salary of $48 a week, Parks became a rich man. In the same three years, he spent $150,000 of union funds on his own pleasures—and no one dared ask questions. Eventually his local union suspended him, but he had enough influence with the national union to have the suspension lifted.

Racketeering was, and is, a two-way street. The employer or employers get something; the racketeer gets something. What Parks did was to help one employer take business from others. In other instances, union racketeers have joined hands with groups of employers for mutual benefit. In 1902, for example, leaders of the teamsters' union in Chicago worked together with the coal association to raise cartage fees from $1.40 to $2 a load. Any coal hauler who did not charge the $2 rate found himself with a strike on his hands—called by business agents of the teamsters' union.

In due course, members of organized crime penetrated the labor movement. Almost always they had the support of employers and politicians. In 1929 the Dailey Commission in Chicago reported that "behind every crooked business agent there was a crooked contractor." As the companies grew richer, union racketeers waxed fat as well. One such union official amassed a number of large companies and a half-million dollar fortune on a salary of $50 a week. When asked how he did it, he replied that "it was with great thrift." This particular business agent sold strike insurance to new contractors for as much as twenty thousand dollars a building. Those who paid the insurance had no fear of strikes being called against them; those who didn't were besieged by strikes.

The take of labor racketeers sometimes ran into six figures. Before being sentenced to jail, Robert F. Bindell amassed a fortune of a million dollars from 1915 to 1920 as the head of New York's building trades unions. This leader of the working class was a bizarre sight when he drove up to his office in a giant limousine with two chauffeurs opening doors and fawning on him.

Contrary to what might be expected, criminals were not unwelcome to some employers. This was especially true in industries where there was cutthroat competition. Harold Seidman, in his book *Labor Czars: A History of Labor Racketeering,* tells how the gangsters under Al Capone brought "order" into the cleaning and dyeing industry of Chicago. The mob dominated not only the main union active in this industry but the Master Cleaners and Dyers Association—the employers' organization—as well. With this leverage, the Capones were able to "advise" small shop owners which master cleaner to patronize and what price to pay. Seidman records that "if shop owners refused to patronize the master cleaners to which they had been assigned by the racket, union truckmen would not pick up their garments." In a sense the mob brought order to a highly competitive, price-cutting industry. The result was probably welcomed by many of the employers. They benefited financially, as did the union racketeers. The people who suffered were the consumers.

Following is an extreme case of union racketeering, which involved both employers and the government.

In 1937, five workers in a Chicago grocery warehouse decided to form a union. They began as an independent union, affiliated with neither the AFL nor the CIO, but eventually received a CIO charter and completed the organization of six hundred employees in their warehouse.

The company, a nationwide grocery chain, refused, however, to recognize the CIO union. The six hundred workers went out on strike and stayed out for almost six months. After a while they decided to extend their strike to the company's retail stores. At the height of the stoppage, fifty of the largest stores were being picketed, in addition to the warehouse. Many customers stayed away, and hundreds of store clerks joined the warehousemen's union.

For a few weeks there were mass picket lines every day, and the company was unable to operate. Soon, however, management signed a contract with an AFL union that had virtually no members at the warehouse and recruited hundreds of new employees. The strike was broken, the CIO union smashed. Long afterward, the National Labor Relations Board reinstated a hundred fifty workers and granted them $51,000 in back pay. By that time, however, everyone was dispersed far and wide. The strike stayed broken.

The seed of unionism, however, began to affect workers in the retail stores. The company began again to look for a way to block the new union campaign. At this point a man named Max Caldwell entered the scene. Son-in-law of the advertising manager of a local AFL paper, Caldwell had once owned a nightclub and had a long record of arrests and at least one six-month jail sentence. He was obviously an unsavory character, but he had somehow wangled a local union charter from the Retail Clerks International Protective Association (RCIPA) of the AFL, and he was ready for business.

Caldwell signed an agreement with the grocery chain even though he had no members. The agreement was one of the shortest on record. Its two paragraphs provided that all clerks would have to join the Caldwell union, and that there would be no wage increase for two years. Subsequently, the agreement was extended for another two years, again without any wage increase.

Caldwell entered into a similar arrangement with two other grocery chains and eventually with companies that employed, all told, twelve thousand workers. In return the racketeer was allowed to exact $2 a month dues from every member, plus initiation fees of $3 to $100. Not a single worker had ever been organized by him prior to the signing of the contracts; none even knew him. Every now and then, Caldwell called membership meetings. But anyone who challenged him, or even asked to see a copy of the contract, was handled roughly. One elderly woman was ousted from the office when she asked about sick benefits, and thrown down the stairs.

When a group of young workers finally organized a successful campaign to remove Caldwell in 1941, the state's attorney found only $62.18 in the union safe. According to the attorney for the dissidents, $910,000 was missing. On a salary of $125 a week, Caldwell then owned two buildings, two private homes in Chicago and Florida, bonds, diamonds, and other possessions. Nothing ever happened to Caldwell or his associates; he had powerful political connections, as well as the support of the chain stores with which he had collaborated.

This had been a beneficial arrangement for both the companies and Caldwell the racketeer. The racketeer got rich, and the companies saved many millions of dollars in wage increases they would have had to pay if there had been a legitimate union. A $2 a week raise for twelve thousand employees comes to about $1¼ million a year. With a democractic union to represent them, these grocery workers could certainly have won at least that much. Thus the companies saved over a million dollars a year as a result of their partnership with a racketeer. And the racketeer himself did not do too badly either.

Not all union racketeering was as brazen as Caldwell's. Usually the racketeer did get some benefits for his members. But his true purpose was to help management—and himself. It was a two-way street.

Bread and Roses

It is we who plowed the prairies;
   built the cities where they trade;
Dug the mines and built the workshops;
   endless miles of railroad laid;
Now we stand, outcast and starving,
   'mid the wonders we have made;
      But the Union makes us strong.

from "Solidarity Forever,"
the union song
written by Ralph Chaplin

Business unionism was one side of the labor story at the beginning of the twentieth century. The other side was the heartrending struggle of women, children, immigrants, miners in the Rockies, and many others for simple elementary justice.

The first decade and a half of this century was called the Progressive Era. After a long period of class conflict, there was an awakening of conscience in America. Writers like Ida Tarbell, Lincoln Steffens, and Upton Sinclair—known as muckrakers—exposed corruption in industry and government.

Twenty-five states enacted legislation limiting the workday, and tens of thousands of working people won a reduction of hours through their unions. Hours of labor for skilled workers fell, by and large, to 49 a week, and for the unskilled to 56. Thirty-eight states passed laws setting age limits and hours of work for chil-

dren. Thirty-five introduced workmen's compensation bills to provide payments for employees injured in industrial accidents. Such
rights did not exist before.

Still, a seamy side existed in the Progressive Era alongside its
sunnier one. There was a bedlam of strikes, antiunion campaigns,
picket line murders, abuse of immigrants, and other downright
cruelty. Nothing, for instance, could have matched the harshness
displayed against hard-rock miners and smeltery workers in the
Colorado Rockies. During their fifteen-month strike at Cripple
Creek, Colorado, in 1903–04, 42 men were killed, 112 wounded,
1,345 held in bull pens for many months without the right of
habeas corpus, and 773 forcibly deported out of the area. General
Sherman Bell, whose state troops were being paid by the employers, refused to obey a judge's order to release prisoners being held
illegally. "To hell with the Constitution!" he cried. "We're not
following the Constitution!"

As late as 1910, 2 million children were still working. Their
average pay in the clothing industry was $2 a week, and in the
glass and silk industries less than $3 a week. Conditions in the
workshops were often horrible. In 1914, thirty-five thousand were
killed on the job and seven hundred thousand injured. "At least
one-half of these deaths were preventable," said the government
Commission on Industrial Relations.

Women in particular worked in gloomy, stench-ridden sweatshops, with inadequate ventilation, heat, or other conveniences.
At one of these sweatshops, the Triangle Shirtwaist Company on
New York City's East Side, 147 Jewish and Italian immigrant
women met their death in 1911 as fire consumed their three-story
factory. They found themselves unable to break through steel
doors their employer had locked to prevent them from going to
the toilet too often. Many jumped to their death.

During the Progressive Era, a new wave of union organization
swept the country. The AFL grew to 2 million members as all
kinds of new workers joined its fold. Militant Jewish workers,
most of them fresh from Czarist Russia where they had developed

Breaker boys, operators of a machine for breaking coal at the Pennsylvania Coal Company, 1911   PHOTO BY LEWIS HINE/LIBRARY OF CONGRESS

a strong tradition of unionism—and socialism—formed unions in the needle trades, together with Italian immigrants. In 1909, twenty thousand shirtwaist workers—80 percent of them women —went on strike in New York; a year later, sixty thousand needle trades workers struck and won a collective bargaining agreement.

With these victories under its belt, the International Ladies' Garment Workers' Union (ILGWU), established ten years before, spread out to Chicago, Cleveland, and Boston; by 1920, it had a hundred thousand members. In 1910, a successful strike against the Hart Schaffner & Marx men's clothing company in Chicago

◀A young driver at a West Virginia mine, 1908   PHOTO BY LEWIS HINE/LIBRARY OF CONGRESS

laid the groundwork for the formation of the Amalgamated Clothing Workers.

The mild tenor of the AFL, however, didn't seem to suit the tough former cowboys, hunters, prospectors, and trappers who had settled in places like Coeur d'Alene, Idaho, or Telluride, Colorado, and were now working in hard-rock mines. They had formed a new federation in 1893, the Western Federation of Miners, which in turn became the core of the most radical union federation in American history, the Industrial Workers of the World (IWW).

Established in 1905 under the leadership of a hulking miner named William D. "Big Bill" Haywood, the IWW proclaimed that "the working class and the employing class have nothing in common." Like the AFL, the IWW was composed of national unions. Unlike the AFL, however, it was an industrial union—all its members were grouped by industry rather than craft. All brewery workers were in one union, all miners in another, all textile workers in a third, and so on. Unskilled workers, white and black, were grouped with skilled craftsmen in the same organization. And whereas the goal of the AFL was simple—to achieve day-to-day objectives ("more")—the goal of the IWW was to prepare workers for revolution through strikes for higher wages. Eventually, it was hoped, all workers in the country would call a general strike, fire the capitalists, and run the factories and mines themselves.

No group captured the mood of the early century like the Wobblies, as the IWW members were called. Whether one agrees with their methods or not, they were the most colorful union members in American history. They answered fire with fire, gunshot with gunshot, and wore overalls as a badge of honor. They rode the rods (of freight trains), tramped the roads, marched off to jail defiantly. They fought and they sang, and their songs had the bite and tang of America.

They sang about "long-haired preachers" who promised "pie in the sky." They called the moderate American Federation of Labor, the American Separation of Labor. And they talked scornfully of "Scissor Bill" who "wouldn't join the union" and of "Casey Jones, the Union Scab." Their songs were often based on old religious songs but had a radical twist. Thus the lyrics of "Dump the Bosses Off Your Back" were written by John Brill to the music of "Take It to the Lord in Prayer." Their most famous song, "Solidarity Forever," is still the anthem of labor unions today, sung during strikes and demonstrations. The Wobblies were for one big union, one big strike of all the workers in the country, which would overthrow capitalism.

The Wobblies never had their revolution, but they did lead numerous militant strikes, as well as hundreds of fights for free speech. When certain cities refused to permit unionists or radicals to hold meetings, the Wobblies would send out a call to members all over the country. Hundreds would come by foot and freight train. A soapbox would be put up in the center of town and a Wobbly would rise to speak. As he was hauled off to jail by the police, another would take his place. Finally when the jails were full and the city taxpayers became concerned over the cost of feeding the prisoners, the police would relent and permit free speech. At Spokane, Washington, five hundred Wobblies submitted to arrest in this manner. At Fresno, San Diego, Kansas City, and many other cities, a similar pattern was followed.

The Wobblies were excellent organizers; they won far more strikes than they lost. To list all of them would take many pages, but the one that typified their efforts was a strike of twenty-three thousand textile workers in Lawrence, Massachusetts, in 1912.

Lawrence, an industrial city thirty miles north of Boston, had a population of eighty-six thousand in 1912 and was known as the worsted center of the world. It was a one-industry town, made up of twelve woolen and cotton mills, with thirty-two thousand workers, most of them immigrants from Italy, French Canada, Poland, Russia, Lithuania, Syria, and twenty other countries. With their children, these immigrants comprised 86 percent of the population.

Wages, even by 1912 levels, were exceptionally poor. For 56

hours of work a week, the average pay was $8.76. Half of that went for rent. A five-room flat in the most congested part of town, with the toilet in the hallway, rented for $4 a week. According to a U.S. Senate report, a normal family of five had to have two members working in order to exist. Most families had to take in boarders to add a pittance to their income.

"Often," one witness told a congressional committee, "the children went hungry. There were days when only bread and water kept them alive." Walter Weyl, an adviser to former President Theodore Roosevelt, reported that he had "rarely seen in any American city so many shivering men without overcoats as I have seen in the cloth-producing town of Lawrence." Of every 1,000 infants, 172 died before the age of one. Company profits were quite good. Dividends of the largest company, American Woolen, were twice as high in 1911 as in 1902.

The strike began after a new law reduced the work schedule for women and children from 56 hours a week to 54, and the companies refused to pay the workers for those 2 hours. Thus, what was supposed to be an improvement in the textile workers' conditions turned out to be, in effect, 2 hours' cut in pay. Two years earlier, when weekly hours had been reduced from 58 to 56, the operatives had been paid the same amount for the shorter workweek. This time, however, shorter hours meant less pay.

On January 11, as the pay envelopes were being passed around at the Everett Cotton Mill, Polish weavers counted their money and began shouting "Not enough pay, not enough pay." Company men who spoke Polish tried to explain that since they had worked only 54 hours, they were entitled to only 54 hours' pay. But the women were not appeased—their paychecks were 32 cents short. They sat at their machines and refused to work.

By nightfall the 1,750 operatives had determined they wouldn't go back unless they got the 32 cents. The same decision was arrived at by 100 workers at a second mill. The next morning, the fury spread from one mill to another. Italian workers at American Woolen's Washington mill shouted that had been cheated out of "four loaves of bread," and roamed from room to room shutting off electricity, cutting belts, smashing light bulbs, and threatening those who would not leave their machines. "Better to starve fighting," they shouted, "than to starve working."

By 11:30 A.M. the mill was shut. From the Washington mill, the strikers, with Italian and American flags flying, marched to another and then still another mill, repeating the process and inflicting damage. A few workers were hurt, six strikers were arrested, various machinery was smashed, and windows were broken. But despite the violence, there were ten thousand men, women, and children on strike.

Unions were weak in Lawrence. The AFL's United Textile Workers of America had a small local union of skilled mule-spinners. There were also nine independent unions, representing better-paid English-speaking craftsmen. The IWW's Local 20 claimed a thousand members, of whom only three hundred had paid their dues. In an industry with thirty-two thousand workers, the total number of union members before the strike was amazingly small. And none of the unions, including the IWW, had played a role in initiating the strike. It was spontaneous.

Once the work stoppage began, the strikers realized they needed help—to form picket lines, deal with the press, raise money for relief, call out workers from other factories, conduct mass meetings. Sam Gompers of the AFL was not particularly sympathetic to the strike. The local AFL affiliate not only refused to permit its skilled craftsmen to join the stoppage but actively tried to keep them on the job, in the hope that the employers would then recognize and deal with the AFL. Its leader called the strikers anarchists. Thus with no help to be expected from the AFL, the strikers, meeting at the Franco-Belgian Hall, voted to send a telegram to Joseph J. "Smiling Joe" Ettor, a member of the IWW executive board, asking him to come to Lawrence and help them.

Smiling Joe arrived in town on Saturday afternoon, in time to address a mass meeting. Only twenty-seven years old, short, husky, and with a ready smile, he was considered one of the most brilliant tacticians in the labor movement. Born of radical Italian parents and raised in Chicago, he worked as an ironworker in San

Francisco and joined the Socialist party, then the IWW. He was an excellent soapbox speaker. If he didn't look like a typical worker—with his immaculate blue suit, Windsor tie, and hat tilted to the side—he nonetheless cast a magnetic spell on working people. He could speak English, Polish, and Italian fluently, and get along in Yiddish and Hungarian. In this first speech, he told the Lawrence workers: "Make this strike as peaceful as possible. In the last analysis, all the blood spilled will be your blood."

Accompanying Ettor was Arturo Giovannitti, a tall, robust man, also under thirty, who was a recent convert to the Wobblies and editor of *Il Proletario,* newspaper of the Italian Socialist Federation. Where Ettor was practical, Giovannitti was romantic, poetic. Ettor took charge of the strike; Giovannitti was assigned to strike relief: getting food, clothing, and money for the strikers.

Ettor's first order of business was to form a strike committee. Four workers were elected by each of the fourteen largest ethnic groups, forming the committee of fifty-six that ran the strike. "Never before," noted the New York *Sun,* "has a strike of such magnitude succeeded in uniting in one unflinching, unyielding, determined, and united army as large and diverse a number of human beings."

The main job of the committee was the organization of large-scale picketing. Thousands of strikers and friends walked in front of the mills twenty-four hours a day, carrying placards with messages such as DON'T BE A SCAB and calling on friends to join them. One of the picket signs expressed the view of women workers: WE WANT BREAD AND ROSES TOO.

Within a week after the mass picketing began, the number of workers on strike reached twenty-two thousand. Most of the workers were recruited by persuasion; but some were intimidated by the big picket lines, and a few were physically stopped. There was no question, however, that the strikers had the support of an overwhelming majority of the operatives—and the public.

The corporations, headed by the American Woolen Company's

William Wood, saw immediately that their first task was to halt or severely reduce the picketing. They had the support of local and state authorities.

On the Monday after Ettor came to town, the first confrontation took place. As pickets, moving from one plant to another, tried to cross bridges over a canal, police and militia blasted them with water from high pressure hoses. Thirty-six strikers were arrested, twenty-nine charged with rioting or carrying dangerous weapons.

It wasn't much of a war as yet, though the newspapers, including *The New York Times,* falsely reported that there had been a "bayonet charge." The picketing, however, continued. Every few days, the strike committee conducted parades, ranging from three thousand to ten thousand participants, marching through the center of town with flags flying, bands playing, and workers singing "Solidarity Forever" or the Socialist "Internationale." "It was the first strike I ever saw which sang," wrote Ray Stannard Baker.

To supplement mass picketing, small committees visited the homes of scabs, and if they couldn't convince them to join the strike, daubed their walls with the word *scab.* Though twenty-five hundred troops were called to the scene, plus private Pinkerton detectives and police, the number of strikers continued to swell. On January 19, a thousand skilled workers, most of them American-born, joined the work stoppage.

Meanwhile the police and courts were doing everything they could to throttle the picketing. Hundreds of strikers were arrested, some sentenced to as long as a year, others fined. Toward the end of January, the state militia was put in full charge, and one of its first acts was to forbid picketing, parades, or demonstrations by three or more people. Owen R. Lovejoy of the National Conference of Charities and Correction said that militiamen he interviewed frankly admitted that they "were fighting on the side of the mill owners" to break the strike.

Yet the picketing continued. Groups of a few dozen linked arms and walked along a sidewalk. Similar groups invaded stores, creating turmoil but using no violence. Police often clubbed and sometimes bayoneted pickets. One pregnant Italian woman conceived of the idea of forming a picket line of pregnant strikers, on the theory that police would not dare attack pregnant women. She was wrong. The police beat the pickets so badly that two of them lost their babies and almost lost their lives. But the marching continued; it was simply impossible to suppress more than twenty thousand active people who marched and sang constantly about "the good old picket line."

Since neither Local 20 nor the IWW's National Industrial Union of Textile Workers had any money, the strikers appealed to friends everywhere for help. An average of a thousand dollars a day came in, sometimes as much as three thousand dollars. Fifteen relief stations were opened, as well as soup kitchens that fed twenty-three hundred pickets a day. Families were given $2 to $5.50 a week for food, and $1 for coal and 50 cents for wood every two weeks. Two volunteer doctors provided medical care.

On January 25, Governor Eugene N. Foss urged both parties to declare a 30-day truce and accept arbitration. The strike committee, however, refused to consider it. Wobblies did not believe in arbitration as a means of settling strikes. Twice, Ettor and a committee of five met with President Wood of the American Woolen Company, but Wood refused to budge.

On January 29, the companies tried to reopen their mills. The strikers formed a massive picket line. Though there was some violence, Joe Ettor, at the head of the line, constantly urged his followers to avoid confrontation. When the police stopped the marchers on the main street, Ettor led them into side streets. Nonetheless an ugly mood built up, some strikers throwing stones at streetcars carrying scabs. *The New York Times* reported: Real Labor War Now in Lawrence.

In the evening, police set up barricades. Strikers threw chunks of coal and snowballs at the police. After a police sergeant was hit, he ordered the police to draw their guns. One policeman, identified by nineteen strikers as Oscar Benoit, fired and killed an Italian striker named Anna Lo Pizzo. The government claimed that Lo Pizzo was killed by two union sympathizers, and seized Ettor and Giovannitti as accessories—even though neither of them had been anywhere near the picket line that evening. The two strike leaders were held in jail for the next eight months.

The mill owners and the authorities evidently believed that the strike would collapse once its leaders were jailed. But this was not the case. When the courts refused to grant bail for Ettor and Giovannitti, IWW leader Bill Haywood came to Lawrence to take charge of the strike, assisted by a team of other national officers.

Meanwhile, martial law was imposed by the city government, twelve more militia companies were called in, street gatherings of three or more were forbidden, and Colonel E. LeRoy Sweetser became, for all practical purposes, the ruler of Lawrence. The town's mill district soon resembled a city awaiting war. Arrests, teargassing, and harassment skyrocketed. Even nonstrikers were driven from the street. An eighteen-year-old Syrian boy, member of the strikers' drum and bugle corps, was bayoneted to death by militiamen as he tried to run away from them.

Bayonets, as Haywood and Ettor pointed out frequently, could not weave cloth. The number of strikebreakers—usually seven thousand or eight thousand—fell to its lowest point, and the number of strikers reached its peak.

Big Bill Haywood, the one-eyed giant who had recently been acquitted of a false murder charge in Idaho (Wobblies and Socialists called it a frame-up), was internationally known and a hero to radicals and unionists around the country. He was also, like Ettor, an excellent organizer. When the authorities forbade picketing individual mills, he had the pickets form an endless chain, sometimes with as many as ten thousand pickets, which marched on sidewalks without stopping. It was not possible to sweep everyone off the sidewalks without silencing the whole city's business. Thus for the next month, the stalemate continued.

During this time a sensational development occurred which won considerable public support for the strikers. On February 5, the Italian Socialist Federation in New York offered to place children of Lawrence's strikers in foster homes, so they could be better fed and housed during the stoppage. On February 10, 119 children, ages four to fourteen, accompanied by 4 women, made their way from Lawrence to Grand Central Station in New York City. A week later, 126 more emaciated children were shipped out, most of them to New York City, 35 to Barre, Vermont. The exodus raised tempers, pro and con, everywhere. Fashionable Beacon Hill ladies predicted that such children in time would become "veritable breeders of anarchy." By and large, however, the exodus brought immense support and publicity for the strikers throughout the country, and hostility toward the woolen corporations.

On February 22, Lawrence's police chief announced that no more children would be allowed to leave. Seven tots who were headed to Connecticut that day were placed in a paddy wagon and taken to a police station, and their parents were told the city would provide for them.

The climax came two days later when two hundred children were scheduled to depart for Philadelphia. Most parents withdrew their children out of fear the police would hold them, just as they had done before. But forty youngsters and their parents did show up. Police and militia barred the way, and when the children, lined up two by two, began to walk to the train, the police began swinging their clubs left and right. Mothers and children were dragged to a military truck and clubbed still again. Thirty adults and youngsters were arrested on the charge of "congregation"; fourteen children were sent to the city farm by the juvenile courts.

News of the event sent shock waves throughout the nation. "It's an outrage," said America's leading literary figure, William Dean Howells. Progressive U.S. senators joined the chorus demanding an investigation of events in Lawrence, and such well known figures as Mrs. William Howard Taft, wife of the president, journeyed to the strike scene to observe matters for themselves. Scores of reporters and writers came to the textile city to make their own estimates.

Under the prodding of Victor Berger of Milwaukee, a Socialist member of the House of Representatives, Congress ordered a

During the 1912 textile workers strike in Lawrence, Massachusetts, children of the strikers aroused great public sympathy when they were sent to New York and other cities so they could have adequate food and housing.   BROWN BROTHERS

probe. The Strike Committee in Lawrence sent sixteen adolescents to the preliminary hearing, to give the strikers' side of the story. One of the high points of the hearing was the testimony of Camella Teoli, age fourteen, who told how she was recruited for a job at the American Woolen Mill even though she had then been under the legal age—fourteen. On her second week at the job, her hair got caught in a machine and "pulled the scalp off." She had been in the hospital seven months, she said, and was still under treatment. Why did she strike? she was asked. "Because I didn't get enough to eat at home," Camella replied.

The negative publicity from the hearings in Washington, as well

William D. "Big Bill" Haywood, leader of the Industrial Workers of the World   LIBRARY OF CONGRESS

as the fact that orders were piling up, finally forced the corporations to give in. After nine and a half weeks of the strike, William Wood of American Woolen finally agreed to wage increases of 5 to 21 percent. The 21 percent went to the lowest paid workers, who received 9½ cents an hour. Other improvements included time and a quarter for overtime, a pledge to reinstate all strikers, and of course the 54-hour week.

On March 14, when fifteen thousand workers met to ratify the agreement, Big Bill Haywood told them "you have demonstrated that there is a common interest in the working class that can bring all its members together." The meeting ended with the singing of the "Internationale."

There was one piece of unfinished business for the strikers— Ettor and Giovannitti were still in jail. As the ratification meeting adjourned, the strikers agreed to focus all their efforts on freeing them. An Ettor-Giovannitti Defense Committee was formed. On May 1, five thousand Lawrence textile workers marched past the prison where the two IWW members were being held. They carried a banner: IF ETTOR AND GIOVANNITTI ARE TO DIE, TWENTY MILLION WORKING MEN WILL KNOW THE REASON WHY. Protest meetings were held not only in America, but in Germany, Sweden, Italy, and France, where some proposed a boycott of American woolen goods and a strike against ships headed for the United States. Giovannitti was nominated in three districts of Italy for the Italian Chamber of Deputies.

On September 30, as the trial of the two men was to begin, twelve thousand textile workers walked out of the mills in a twenty-four-hour protest strike. The police again clubbed strikers and arrested some, and the companies fired fifteen hundred. Haywood had to threaten another general strike to get them reinstated.

The trial lasted fifty-eight days. Both men were acquitted.

The 1919 Steel Strike

Corporations . . . are fast becoming
the people's masters.
President Grover Cleveland

The most serious problem confronting the American labor movement at the beginning of this century was the growth of mass production industries.

In earlier days, companies were relatively small, and people measured their wealth in hundreds of thousands of dollars rather than in millions and tens of millions. But with the great economic spurt that followed the Civil War, business changed. Individual ownership and partnership were increasingly replaced by the impersonal corporation. Many tycoons of industry swallowed up competitors or forced them into mergers. In 1899 alone, ninety-two corporate trusts were launched, including Standard Oil of New Jersey. The 1900 census showed a concentration of capital that two generations earlier would have been considered impossible. One hundred and eighty-five corporations, with a capital of

$3 billion, controlled one-third of all the manufacturing resources of the nation.

In 1901 the banking firm of J. P. Morgan merged twelve steel firms into the United States Steel Corporation, a $1.4 billion conglomerate. With almost ¼ million employees, Big Steel—as it was called—built 90 percent of the nation's bridges; produced half of its pig iron, steel rails, and coke; 60 percent of its structural steel; and nearly all of its barbed wire, wire nails, and tin plate.

The AFL, with its moderate philosophy and meager resources, was unable to match the power of such a giant. The Amalgamated Association of Iron, Steel and Tin Workers, an AFL affiliate, tried twice to come to terms with U.S. Steel on the issue of long hours, but both times was rebuffed and defeated in strikes. The giant trust ordered its affiliates not to deal with unions under any circumstances.

Along with the concentration of capital, there was also a breathtaking advance in industrial technology. Henry Ford, one of the early auto pioneers, proved that producing interchangeable parts and assembling them on an assembly line was far superior to the old method in which each skilled mechanic did many jobs. The linking of electricity with machinery and the power-driven conveyor belt made mass production even more efficient. With the same number of workers, twice as much could be manufactured in 1929 as in 1919.

The result was an explosion of factories with thousands of workers under a single roof. The corporation continued to need skilled workers for certain tasks, such as tool and die making, but the proportion of skilled to unskilled became ever smaller.

The AFL was not designed to deal with corporations so big or with semiskilled or unskilled laborers. Consider the meat-packing industry. As late as 1870, the pioneers of meat-packing, Philip Armour, Gustavus Swift, and Nelson Morris, were still slaughtering cattle only in winter months. They had not yet discovered a means of refrigeration other than natural ice. Armour's firm was then valued at a mere two hundred thousand dollars.

A number of major developments changed all that. One was the construction of the three-hundred-acre Union Stock Yards in Chicago, with facilities for unloading five hundred cattle cars at the same time. An even more important advance was the design by one of Swift's engineers of a freight car that used the principle of air circulation for refrigeration. That made it possible to ship dressed meat all year round.

By 1875 the industry was shipping 250,000 head of cattle a year, and by 1890, 1 million. The plants enlarged apace, introducing division-of-labor methods. The typical worker until then was the skilled butcher, proficient in a dozen tasks that he performed by himself. Now the work was subdivided into 120 separate operations, two-thirds of them performed by unskilled workers along a chain, much like the future assembly lines in automobile factories.

Unfortunately the Amalgamated Meat Cutters and Butcher Workmen of the AFL was not designed to represent assembly-line workers. The union had been fashioned for the horse-and-buggy days of the industry, before it had become mechanized. Instead of one big union for the whole industry, the meat cutters had chartered fifty-six local unions in packinghouse plants. Each one represented a single department, had its own executive board and business agents, and bargained separately.

In 1904, fifty thousand stockyard workers in nine cities responded to a strike call, seeking a minimum wage of 18½ cents an hour. They stayed out for nine weeks and were shot at, clubbed, and arrested by the score. After the second week, their clashes with police and strikebreakers (fourteen hundred of them black workers imported from the South) were daily and violent occurrences. When the strike was defeated, union membership fell from fifty-six thousand to seven thousand.

The Wobblies—militant advocates of industrial unionism and direct action—did have some success with industrial organization. In 1906 the IWW conducted the first sitdown strike in American history, at the General Electric plant in Schenectady, New York.

The Wobblies didn't win this one, but three years later at the

Pressed Steel Car plant in McKees Rock, Pennsylvania—six miles from Pittsburgh—they fared better. After a number of violent clashes in which a deputy sheriff, two strikebreakers, and eight strikers were killed, the company agreed to 15 percent wage increases and the rehiring of all strikers. It was a resounding victory for the IWW.

The Wobblies, however, though excellent strike organizers, were poor at holding an organization together after strikes were won. One of the reasons was that they were opposed in principle to requiring all workers to belong to the union—a closed shop; they believed in voluntarism and persuasion. They felt the worker should belong to a union and pay dues because he wanted to, not because a union contract said he had to. It was an excellent idea —in theory—and it worked well in European countries where a majority of workers were Socialists. But it didn't work in the United States. The Wobblies failed to unionize mass production workers. Someone else had to do it.

The task fell to a former Wobbly, William Z. Foster, who came forth with a new strategy, called amalgamation, which he felt would make the AFL itself effective in dealing with the big steel moguls.

Foster was an interesting figure. One of twenty-three children born to Irish immigrant parents, he was tall, wiry, good-looking, and immensely resourceful. In 1894, at the age of thirteen, Foster was clubbed down by police during a strike of Philadelphia streetcar men. In 1901, just twenty, he joined the newly formed Socialist party. Eight years later, after three years at sea and while serving a two-month sentence in Spokane, Washington, where the Wobblies were conducting a free-speech fight, Foster joined the IWW. His arrest had been the first of many—in Kansas City, Missoula, Newark, Chicago, Denver, New York, and in eight Pennsylvania towns during the 1919 steel strike. Eventually Foster would become the leader of the American Communist party; but in the decade after 1910, he flirted with all kinds of political nostrums.

Early in that decade, Foster, though still devoted to the radicalism of the Wobblies, decided that radicals ought to work within the AFL to transform it, not outside. He took a job as car inspector on the Soo Line, joined Local 453 of the Brotherhood of Railway Carmen, and became its delegate to the Chicago Federation of Labor (CFL). He was obviously well liked, for he was chosen business agent for the thirteen carmen local unions; and when he refused a second term, he was unanimously asked to reconsider.

It was as a delegate to the Chicago Federation of Labor that Foster teamed up with John Fitzpatrick, the CFL president, to organize meat-packing workers. While walking to work in July 1917, Foster conceived of an ingenious plan that was a cross between craft and industrial unionism. He called it amalgamation, or federated unionism. It would permit the craft organizations to continue their separate existence, but would federate them into a single packinghouse council, with its own executive board and business agents.

The council in effect would function like an industrial union, but the members it recruited would pay dues to separate craft unions. A few days after he conceived the idea, Foster sold it to his own carmen and then, with Fitzpatrick's help, had it endorsed by the CFL.

Thus was born the Stockyard Labor Council, with representatives from a dozen unions, including the Butcher Workmen, Railway Carmen (who produced the refrigerated freights), Carpenters, Machinists, and Steamfitters.

Employees of the industry hadn't received a raise for thirteen years; they were ripe for unionism. And though Foster and Fitzpatrick enjoyed only lukewarm support from the AFL leadership and the butcher workmen's national union, they succeeded beyond their wildest dreams. Thousands flocked to the amalgamated union. When Foster threatened a nationwide strike, the matter was referred by Samuel Gompers to the Federal Mediation Commission. Its ruling, in December 1917, was all that Foster and Fitzpatrick could hope for: a 10 percent raise and seniority rights.

(Seniority rights guarantee that when there is to be a layoff, the senior employee stays on the job and the employee with least seniority is laid off. The senior employee is also entitled to other benefits.) In a subsequent arbitration, the amalgamated union won other concessions for the 125,000 meat-packing workers—an 8-hour workday with the same 10 hours' pay, plus additional raises of 10 to 25 percent. "It's a new day," Fitzpatrick told jubilant workers in Chicago.

Encouraged by the results in the meat-packing industry, Foster turned his attention to the most important mass production industry in the country: steel. No one had to tell Foster he would be facing a powerful adversary. U.S. Steel alone employed ¼ million workers. Its board chairman, Judge Elbert Henry Gary—for whom Gary, Indiana, is named—was also president of the American Iron and Steel Institute. He was to be Foster's main adversary.

Judge Gary believed that responsibility for the welfare of working people must be left to "the employers, the capitalists, those having the highest education, the greatest power and influence," not to outside unions. To offset the influence of outsiders, Gary spent $65 million from 1912 to 1919 to improve the lot of U.S. Steel workers. He built recreational facilities, offered options to buy stocks, introduced accident prevention measures and improved sanitation, and built 25,964 housing units. Other firms didn't adopt such paternalistic measures, but they organized company-controlled unions and allowed workers to air their grievances through those "unions." From the turn of the century to August 1918, the steel companies had granted seven general raises, more than doubling the pay scales for common labor.

But none of this appeased the steelworkers. Their loudest cry was for an 8-hour day. Wartime steel business was booming, and the industry's workers were required to work long hours. Half of them labored 12 hours a day, six days a week. Every second week, when they changed from day to night shifts, there was a "long turn" of 18 to 24 hours without rest. Some put in 11 hours of work on the day shift one week, 13 on the night shift the following week. Less than 25 percent were lucky enough to toil less than 60 hours a week.

The Senate Committee on Education and Labor called "the policy of working men 10 and 12 hours per day in the steel mills" an "unwise and un-American policy." The wage policy, too, was not as favorable as it seemed. Some skilled workers, it is true, earned $20 and $30 a day—a very high wage in 1918. But even though the wages of common laborers had more than doubled, so too had prices in the war years.

All signs indicated that steelworkers were ready to unionize. Foster was sure a six-week "hurricane drive" would unionize the whole industry. The AFL had plenty of money by this time. His own union, the Railway Carmen, had $3 million in its treasury. All that was needed was a bit of daring and vision. Foster proposed that twenty-four craft unions, each expecting to get a share of 500,000 steelworkers as members, form a federation. The local unions in any given area, regardless of what national union they came from, would form an iron and steelworkers' council to do the actual organizing; and a national committee, with Foster and Fitzpatrick in charge, would coordinate matters.

In September 1918, while World War I was still on, Foster began his drive in four cities around Chicago: Joliet, Gary, South Chicago, and Indiana Harbor. He borrowed organizers from the more progressive AFL unions, such as the United Mine Workers, and he ultimately assembled a staff of a hundred organizers. The results were sensational. Fifteen thousand steelworkers attended the first meeting in Gary, and 749 paid their initiation fee on the spot. Within a month, the federation of steel unions had enough members to fully paralyze all the mills in the Chicago area, if it wanted to. Foster didn't call his strike at this time because the hub of the industry was around Pittsburgh and Youngstown. Shutting down the Chicago area would not be enough.

Alarmed by the union drive, Judge Gary put into effect a "basic 8-hour day" with time and a half after 8 hours. This did not reduce the workday—since the men still had to labor 12 hours—but it did add 2 hours' pay every day to the paycheck.

Encouraged by this victory—no small achievement for a one-month campaign—Foster moved his headquarters to Pittsburgh. Organizers fanned out along the Monongahela River and to steel towns in Ohio and West Virginia. Those areas, however, proved more difficult to unionize than Chicago. Judge Gary and his allies put up stiff resistance. Their first effort at obstruction was to make it difficult, if not impossible, for the union to get a place to meet.

In a dozen cities of Pennsylvania, company-minded mayors and town councils passed ordinances requiring permits for mass meetings, which they then refused to issue or held up. Foster's National Committee reported in July 1919 that McKeesport had finally granted a permit for a meeting after considering it for seven months. But Clairton and Duquesne "still refuse to allow the American Federation of Labor to hold any meeting." Obviously it was difficult to unionize steelworkers if you couldn't meet with them.

Foster defied the ban on free speech by forming flying squadrons of ten organizers each to invade various steel towns. They were repeatedly arrested, but they repeatedly came back. The organizing committee also appealed to miners nearby, and in April 1919, ten thousand members of the United Mine Workers marched into Monessen, a steel town forty miles from Pittsburgh. With that kind of muscle, their meeting went on as scheduled.

Little by little, democracy returned to Pennsylvania, but not entirely. In August a forty-nine-year-old grandmother, Fannie Sellins, was killed by "peace officers" at West Natrona when she tried to remove children from the scene of a meeting. A deputy pumped a bullet into her body as she lay on the ground; no one was ever prosecuted for that act. The same month, authorities in Duquesne denied a permit for a meeting to be addressed by the nationally known rabbi Stephen Wise. "Jesus Christ himself could not speak in Duquesne for the AFL," said the town's mayor. Thousands of workers were fired for joining the union, and

Foster was denounced in the media as a rip-roaring communist.

With all that, however, 100,000 steelworkers had joined the union by June 1919, and more were coming in daily. At the end of the drive, Foster reported that 156,702 workers had paid initiation fees, and 100,000 more had signed application cards for the union. About half the industry was now enrolled for the campaign for "8 hours and the union." But Judge Gary refused to consider recognizing the union. A letter from Samuel Gompers, asking Gary to meet with a committee of six, including himself and Foster, went unanswered. With thousands of its members being fired and no signs from management of a willingness to talk, the National Committee decided to strike in late September. President Woodrow Wilson appealed for a two-week postponement, but the appeal came a day or two after police had killed three strikers engaged in a work stoppage at the Standard Steel Company of Hammond, Indiana.

The steel strike of 1919 was part of an immense strike wave that included a city-wide walkout in Seattle, a work stoppage by Boston police, and strikes in the coal and clothing industries—altogether more than four thousand walkouts.

The steel strike, however, was the most important. As it began, it resembled mobilization for a real war. Thousands of men were recruited in Pittsburgh as deputy sheriffs, and three thousand more at McKeesport. Along the Monongahela River, in towns from Pittsburgh to Clairton, twenty-five thousand men were selected, armed, and paid by the steel corporations but called deputies so they could claim official authority. The deputies were to serve two purposes: to prevent workers from leaving their jobs and to protect strikebreakers.

On a Sunday, state police rode their horses into a crowd of three thousand steelworkers and their families at North Clairton. Many were clubbed, kicked, and injured; sixteen were arrested on the charge of disorderly conduct. Police and deputies mounted similar attacks against strike meetings in literally scores of places. Foster produced hundreds of affidavits citing criminal behavior by deputies, but neither the governor of Pennsylvania nor President Wilson intervened to restore civil liberties in the steel towns.

A worker at Homestead related how state police had invaded his home without a warrant while he was asleep, kicked him, and took him half-naked to jail. The next day he was fined $15.10. At Monessen, state police rounded up groups of foreign-born strikers at the mill gates. Those who said they were willing to go to work were freed; the others were jailed in rickety buildings and threatened with hanging. The sheriff of Allegheny County prohibited outdoor meetings of more than three people, and ruled that indoor meetings could be held only if they received official sanction and were conducted in English.

In practice, of course, meetings were not permitted in any language in places along forty-one miles of the Monongahela—the very heart of the industry. Mass meetings of strikers and business meetings of union officials were proclaimed illegal. During the whole three and a half months of the strike, almost no meetings of any kind were held in this area.

Yet, despite the corporations and government, the response to the strike was impressive. On September 22, Foster reported 275,000 men had walked out. By the end of the week, according to the U.S. Department of Labor, 367,000 men and women were on strike in seventy major centers. In the Chicago and Buffalo areas, the stoppage was 100 percent effective. Even in the Pittsburgh area, three-quarters of the mill hands had left their jobs.

Judge Gary's counterattack consisted of a combination of fear and force. Mayor John A. Toomey of Buffalo denounced the strike as an attempt by "bolsheviks" to spread the "red" doctrine among foreigners. The Chicago *Tribune* reported in its strike story that "Foster's plan of a social revolution is revealed."

Propaganda, however, was mixed with violence, even on the first day of the strike. Near the American Steel & Wire plant in Farrell, Pennsylvania, one striker and one strikebreaker were killed, and two state troopers injured. At New Castle, seven unionists were shot. All told, twenty-two people would die in the long strike, twenty of them strikers; hundreds were injured, and many hundreds more jailed.

On the fourth day of the stoppage, John Fitzpatrick offered to send the strikers back to work if the company would agree to arbitration—having the issue decided by an impartial third party. Judge Gary scorned the offer; the newspapers played it down as insignificant. Instead they carried fictitious stories of workers returning to work and the morale of strikers sagging. Detective agencies started whispering campaigns pitting one group of foreign workers against another. The Sherman Service, for instance, sent a memo to its agents: "We want you to stir up as much bad feeling as you possibly can between the Serbians and Italians. Spread data among the Serbians that the Italians are going back to work. . . . Urge them to go back to work, or the Italians will get their jobs."

The first few weeks of the strike were a stalemate, neither side sure of winning. For a while the owners' back-to-work pleas failed, raising Foster's hopes of ultimate victory.

But the longer the strike lasted, the more remote victory became. "The only way to beat the strikers," Foster observed, "is to starve them out." There was nowhere near enough money to feed them. The twenty-four unions in the amalgamation contributed only $101,000 to the strike fund; other unions, such as the garment workers', men's clothing workers', and furriers', contributed more —$180,000. The AFL itself gave nothing. All told, the strike committee netted $418,000 for strike expenses and relief, hardly enough to feed hundreds of thousands of people.

Foster estimated that he needed $2 million a week for relief, but the best he could do was open forty-five commissariats which distributed food twice a week to those in dire need. The inadequate supply of strike funds was without question the most important factor in the failure of the strike.

After the first few weeks, things began to turn in management's favor. On October 4, strikers returning from a meeting in Gary confronted a small group of blacks, and a minor tussle took place. That was the pretext used by the governor of Indiana to send eleven National Guard companies to Gary and a thousand militiamen to nearby Indiana Harbor.

In vain the union offered to supply seven hundred of its own members, who were war veterans, to keep the peace. A couple of days later, the strikers staged a parade. Thereupon the federal government sent in General Leonard Wood and a regiment from nearby Fort Sheridan, north of Chicago. Strike leaders and pickets were arrested and put to work sweeping streets or splitting wood. Picketing was restricted, union meetings were suppressed, and worst of all, the army itself escorted strikebreakers into the plants.

Black workers turned out to be the largest number of strikebreakers; because blacks had so systematically been excluded from many AFL unions, they felt no kinship for the labor federation. Thirty to forty thousand blacks became strikebreakers in the months that followed.

By the end of October, morale was very low, and some strikers began to return to work. For a brief moment in November, there was a ray of hope: The United Mine Workers had called a strike for a 6-hour day and a 60 percent raise in pay. The steel strike was now six weeks old; if the miners could be persuaded to join with the steelworkers and stay out for a time, the steel companies would run out of coal and have to shut down. The Wilson administration might, under those circumstances, have exerted pressure for a compromise.

But on November 8, Attorney General A. Mitchell Palmer secured an injunction ordering the miners back to work in the bituminous fields. Faced with the injunction, John L. Lewis, new president of the mine union, called off the strike. "We cannot fight the government," he said. (During World War II, twenty-two years later, Lewis and the miners did fight the government and win, refusing to call off their strike until they had an agreement for arbitration that assured them a closed shop in the industry.) Though many miners in 1919 refused to heed Lewis and stayed out for another month, the steel companies were now assured a steady supply of coal.

As of mid-November, the steel mills around Chicago had recruited enough strikebreakers and former strikers to operate at 50 to 85 percent of normal. Everywhere, the ranks were thinning appreciably. Foster and Fitzpatrick tried one more ploy. They asked the Interchurch Commission, representing forty-two Protestant denominations, to contact Judge Gary and settle the strike on any terms it could. On December 5, three nationally respected clergymen met with Judge Gary at his New York office. Gary was unshakable. In fact he accused the commission itself of harboring "red radicals" in its ranks. Concerning the strike, he told them there was nothing to discuss. The steelworkers were back at work and happy, he said. The few that remained out were "nothing but a group of red radicals whom we don't want anyhow."

That was the last gasp of the 1919 steel strike. As of December 10, there were still 109,300 workers out, according to Foster, but the number continued to dwindle rapidly. On January 8, 1920, after three and a half months, the strike was called off, and in July the National Committee for Organizing Iron and Steel Workers was formally dissolved.

The first national strike of mass production workers had been defeated by a combination of government and management strikebreaking, and by hunger in the strikers' homes.

10 Golden Twenties and Turbulent Thirties

Labor, like Israel, has many sorrows.
Its women weep for their fallen,
and they lament for the future of
the children of their race.

John L. Lewis

The decade from 1920 to 1929 was called the Golden Twenties. But it began with the depression of 1920–21, and it ended with the disaster of 1929.

An avalanche of new products swamped the market and created work. The automobile alone provided 4 million jobs in dozens of industries. Telephones moved into the American home. Radio grew from an $11 million industry in 1921 to a $412 million industry eight years later. The electric bulb replaced gaslight, and the electric industry tripled its volume. Companies grew by leaps and bounds. Big corporations merged with other corporations to become even bigger corporations. By 1930 the two hundred largest corporations, excluding banks, controlled half the nation's wealth.

Other changes took place. More people moved to the cities. In

1805, 95 percent of the population had lived in farm areas. By 1920 more than half lived in cities. Immigration was severely reduced as the United States found itself able to supply its own labor force. In the Golden Twenties, only ½ million people emigrated to the United States from Europe.

Unlike the major powers of Europe, the United States had come out of World War I unscathed, with no damage to its industries or cities. It was able to supply other countries with vital goods needed for recovery. Manufacturing production almost doubled during this period.

Yet for working people it was a frustrating decade. In the past, unions had ordinarily declined in bad times and grown in good times. But that didn't happen in the 1920s. Union membership actually declined. AFL ranks fell more than a quarter—from 4 million to less than 3 million. Most of the strikes were defeated, including those of the United Mine Workers, then the most militant union in the country.

During the 1922 stoppage, unions miners attacked a group of strikebreakers at a strip mine near Herrin, Illinois; disarmed the guards; set dynamite to loaded coal cars; and blew up a Bucyrus shovel. Altogether 19 scabs and detectives were killed in what became known as the Herrin Massacre—and 214 unionists were indicted for murder. All union men put on trial were acquitted, but the strike was destined for defeat anyway.

In June the operators offered to reopen the mines at the old wages; the union rejected the offer. A month later, President Warren G. Harding wired twenty-eight governors, asking them to call out the militia to protect the mines—help escort strikebreakers to work.

In August, after eighteen weeks, the leader of the miners, John L. Lewis, made a deal to retain the old wages, and was roundly criticized by the rank and file. In fact, opposition was so fierce that

John L. Lewis, who served as president of both the United Mine ▶ Workers and the Congress of Industrial Organizations   GEORGE MEANY MEMORIAL ARCHIVES/AFL-CIO/LIBRARY OF CONGRESS

branches in six states deserted the union. U.S. Steel bought a hundred thousand acres of mining property in Kentucky and West Virginia, all operated by nonunion miners. The daily wage, which Lewis had originally negotiated for union members, was $7.50 a day; but south of the Ohio River—in Virginia, Kentucky, Tennessee, and Alabama—miners were working in nonunion pits for as little as $3 a day.

Then in 1927, the Pittsburgh Coal Company, which employed 17,000 miners, tore up union agreements, cut pay to $6 a day, and resumed a nonunion open shop. In 1930 the miners' union, which had once reached a peak of 450,000 members, was down to 150,000. At least two-thirds of the nation's coal was now mined by nonunion men.

Wherever one turned after World War I, labor's road was rocky. One hundred thousand cotton mill workers in New England accepted a 20 percent wage cut after seven months on the picket line and many bloody clashes. Sixty-five thousand members of the Amalgamated Clothing Workers in New York fought a six-month battle to maintain a union shop, but had to agree to a 15 percent wage reduction after their strike.

The most important strike of the period involved 400,000 railroad shop craftsmen who were asked to take a cut of 12 percent after a previous cut of 5 to 18 cents an hour. An injunction issued by Judge James H. Wilkerson prohibited union members, their leaders, and their attorneys from writing, speaking, telephoning, or in any way communicating with fellow workers to ask them not to work. Union meetings were barred, and unions were ordered not to spend any money on the strike. Under the weight of that injunction and the failure of the four operating Brotherhoods to help the craftsmen, the stoppage collapsed completely.

Strikebreaking, however, was not the only means used by employers to stymie unions in the Golden Twenties. Thousands of employers of that period concentrated instead on preventing workers from joining unions in the first place. At a January 1921 meeting in Chicago, representatives of manufacturers' associations in twenty-two states vowed that their members would not enter into any agreement with a union.

If harassed by a union, they pledged to help each other keep the union out. They called this the American Plan. Author Savel Zimand observed that "never before has America seen an open shop drive on a scale so vast . . . so heavily financed, so efficiently organized." Capitalizing on the mood of the day, employers who favored the open shop tried to convince their employees that it was unpatriotic, un-American to join a union, that it violated the spirit of free choice.

Corporations formed hundreds of American Plan organizations to promote the idea of an open shop. Thousands of forums were held to denounce the closed shop. By late 1920 there were few places that didn't boast an American Plan organization. All told, employers organized 540 open shop associations to prevent their employees from forming or joining unions. The national Open Shop Association, which coordinated the activities of many of those groups, offered to provide spies and strikebreakers wherever needed to suppress a labor organization.

The head of the Indiana Manufacturers' Association declared "we will not employ an individual in any part of the plant that does not sign an individual contract in which it is expressed that he is not and will not become a member of a labor organization while in our employ." The unions called this a Yellow-Dog Contract. Tens of thousands of workers were forced to sign one—or lose their jobs. Eugene Grace of Bethlehem Steel went a little further; he refused to sell steel to any employer who hired union labor.

Another device used by American Plan advocates to discourage legitimate unions was for companies to form their own so-called unions—company unions. By numerous devices, management controlled these organizations. Usually they were run by a company lawyer or personnel director. By 1927, there were 1.4 million members in hundreds of company unions, but they could neither bargain nor handle grievances as true unions did. In the 1930s Congress finally declared company unions illegal and ordered them dissolved.

By contrast with the Golden Twenties, the 1930s were a depressing decade—certainly in the first few years. But the period witnessed a complete turnaround in labor fortunes.

It all began with the stock market crash of 1929. Shareholders sold their shares in a rising panic. In one day alone, leading stocks dropped $40 to $60 a share. Men who had made fortunes in the previous decade were wiped out overnight, broke. Some committed suicide, jumping from the upper floors of Wall Street skyscrapers.

Things went from bad to worse. Within a few years, 5,761 banks failed; millions of people lost their savings. A million farmers who couldn't pay their mortgages or taxes lost their farms. Factory production declined by half, and construction of new buildings just about stopped. After a while there were 12 million people out of work and millions more working only part-time. Thousands, evicted from their homes, built shacks of cardboard and tin in empty lots or wastelands. They named their communities after President Herbert Hoover—Hoovervilles.

The nation was in the worst depression in its history. Then in March 1933, Franklin D. Roosevelt became president and introduced more changes in one hundred days than any president before him. In order to raise farm prices, farmers were paid to produce less grain than in the past and to kill some of their pigs. Billions were allotted for relief of the unemployed and to create jobs. As of October 1933, 2.5 million unemployed had found work; most of the others were on relief or participating in federal work projects.

Unions too began to recover. The miners' union gambled its $75,000 treasury, hired many organizers, and added more than 300,000 members—jumping from 150,000 to almost 500,000 in a few months. The Ladies' Garment Workers' and the Amalgamated Clothing Workers' unions added almost 250,000 needle trade workers to their ranks. From June to October 1933, 1 million men and women took out union cards.

As the mood of pessimism that had hung over the nation began to vanish, workers everywhere organized and struck to win back old wage scales and benefits. "The country is full of spontaneous strikes," wrote Benjamin Stolberg in December 1933. "Wherever one goes, one sees picket lines."

America was ablaze in class warfare those first few years of Roosevelt's New Deal—and strikers paid a fearsome price for it. From August through October 1933, fifteen strikers were killed on the picket lines. (Another forty suffered the same fate in 1934, and forty-eight more in the next two years.) From mid-1933 to the end of 1934, troops were called out to quell strikes in sixteen of the forty-eight states. Eighteen thousand strikers were arrested from 1934 through 1936, and no one knows how many were injured.

Yet labor achieved its greatest success in the 1930s. It is no exaggeration to say that the high standard of living enjoyed by the American people in subsequent decades was due to victories won in the thirties.

Reversal of the downhill cycle began in 1934 with three big victories—despite one big defeat. The defeat occurred in the textile industry. One of the New Deal laws provided for a National Recovery Administration (NRA) to establish minimum wages for each industry. But the $12- and $13-a-week rates set for textile workers were not being honored by employers.

The United Textile Workers union, which had grown from 50,000 members in 1933 to 300,000 in 1934, called a strike. Three hundred and sixty-five thousand textile workers—many not in the union—responded. They demanded a 30-hour week, the $12 and $13 minimum wages established by the NRA, recognition of the union, and reinstatement of 4,000 unionists fired for union activity. They also wanted an end to the stretch-out—the policy of adding more and more looms for a worker to watch, thus getting more work for the same pay.

The chairman of the union strike committee, Francis J. Gorman, a stocky man in his forties, developed a successful technique for closing southern mills. He formed flying squads to visit non-union mills and get workers to join the strike. After shutting down a factory in one town, the flying squads would proceed to the next town. Needless to say, state governments called out militia to fight the flying squads, and clashes occurred all too frequently.

Finally, however, the strike was called off at the request of President Roosevelt. He agreed to appoint a new board to deal with the textile industry. Strikers, however, gained nothing. In fact, troops prevented workers in hundreds of plants in Georgia and the Carolinas from returning to their jobs. In some factories, strikers had to sign Yellow-Dog Contracts before being admitted back to their looms. Fifteen thousand mill hands never got their jobs back at all.

Three important strikes of 1934, however, ended in big union victories. On May 9, twelve thousand longshoremen on the West Coast (longshoremen load and unload freight vessels) went on strike. Their average wage at the time was $10.45 a week; and to make matters worse, they had to endure the daily humiliation of a "shape-up." The men would "shape-up" around a foreman on the street, and he would pick whomever he wanted to work that day. Thus a longshoreman might work one day and be off for three, or he might agree to work 36 hours without sleep for fear he wouldn't be able to get work later.

The longshoremen, led by a colorful left-wing Australian, Harry Bridges, added a number of new flourishes to strike strategy. The first was determined picketing. One thousand men stood watch at the Embarcadero dock area in San Francisco in 12-hour shifts, day and night. The second was to spread the strike so that it included other maritime workers, such as seamen and teamsters. The third was formation of a Joint Strike Committee, composed of five members from each of the ten unions on strike, with Bridges as chairperson. "It is a different strike from any the Coast has ever known," reported Evelyn Seeley in *The Nation*.

By the time the walkout was seven weeks old, $40 million in wares lay stacked on the piers and ships of San Francisco alone.

Many local industries were beginning to run short of supplies. On July 3, under the leadership of the Industrial Association and supported by the mayor and governor, the companies tried to run strikebreakers through the mass picket line in San Francisco.

For four hours the battle flared, while tens of thousands watched from nearby hills. One picket was killed, several dozen injured. July 3, however, was only a warm-up for July 5, when the Industrial Association tried again. "Don't think of this as a riot," noted the San Francisco *Chronicle*. "It was a hundred riots big and little." Two strikers were killed on this "Bloody Thursday."

The governor sent in seventeen hundred National Guardsmen, and Bridges decided that the strike would have to be expanded or die: "We cannot stand up against police, machine guns, and National Guard bayonets." On July 14, representatives of 115 unions in the Bay Area voted to conduct a general strike; by July 16 and 17, San Francisco and the surrounding areas were in the grips of a full-scale work stoppage—only the third time in U.S. history this sort of thing had happened.

The police and hired vigilantes responded by raiding and demolishing more than a dozen offices, including those of the newspaper of the Communist party. After a few days, the general strike collapsed, but the corporations had had enough. They agreed to an arbitration board; its decision was highly favorable for the strikers. The longshoremen won union recognition, a 30-hour week, a dime an hour raise, and a hiring hall jointly run by the union and employers to replace the shape-up.

Toledo auto workers and Minneapolis warehousemen engaged in work stoppages that were similar in many respects to the San Francisco longshoremen's strike. Again, strikers actively defied government officials.

In Toledo, a work stoppage by four thousand auto workers was on the verge of collapse after a judge issued an order limiting the number of pickets to twenty-five. Eighteen hundred strike breakers were brought into the plant. But an unemployed group, led by radicals of the American Workers party, defied the injunction,

Injured workers receive assistance during the 1934 strike at the Auto-Lite plant in Toledo, Ohio. INTERNATIONAL UNION, UNITED AUTO WORKERS

mobilized thousands of pickets, and resisted both police and National Guardsmen in a running battle that lasted for days. After two strikers were killed and scores of guardsmen sent to the hospital, the company shut the plant. A few days later, as ninety-eight of ninety-nine unions in the city voted for a general strike, management surrendered—recognizing the union and granting a 5 percent raise. The Toledo strike gave impetus to the emergence of the United Auto Workers union (UAW) two or three years later, as the most dynamic labor organization in America.

In Minneapolis, a small organization that followed the teachings of the exiled coleader of the Russian Revolution, Leon

Trotsky, led stoppages by warehousemen and truckers. These strikes made the teamsters' union a major force in American labor. The campaign began when a Trotskyist named Karl Skoglund unionized drivers of coal trucks and quickly won a strike against sixty-seven companies. On the heels of this victory, Teamsters' Local 574 tried to unionize warehouse workers but was rebuffed by management. What followed was a bitter citywide strike in which flying squadrons of pickets roamed the streets, shutting down newspapers, warehouses, gas stations, and markets, and preventing out-of-town trucks from entering the city. Late in May, a big battle—called the Battle of Deputies Run—ensued between police and strikers, in which 20,000 other workers helped the truckers gain a decisive victory. Three days later there was a settlement, and though there was another strike in July and more violence, the union finally succeeded. At the time, the teamsters' union had only 95,000 members nationally; spurred by the Minneapolis strikes, membership grew steadily until it hit a peak of 2 million.

The 1934 strikes gave American labor its first taste of victory in a long time. But the event that made unions a major factor in American life occurred several years later. This was a strike at the nation's General Motors Corporation (GM) plants—a strike that followed a serious split in the labor movement.

In October 1935, the American Federation of Labor broke asunder. The issue of industrial unionism (organizing all the workers in a factory into a single union rather than into many craft unions) could not be sidestepped any longer. Millions of workers were asking to be unionized, but the AFL, with its craft union structure, was not equipped to do it. Among other things, its philosophy was too conservative, and many of its affiliates refused to admit blacks into their ranks.

Under the leadership of John L. Lewis, head of the United Mine Workers, eight national unions established the Committee for Industrial Organization (CIO). They later changed its name to Congress of Industrial Organizations, keeping the initials C. I. O.

The CIO was not a revolutionary union like the Wobblies—
though many of its secondary leaders belonged to the Communist
and other radical parties. But it was not like the old AFL either.
In three years it changed both the character and tone of American
labor.

11 | "Sitdown! Sitdown!"

> When they tie the can to a union man,
>   Sit down! Sit down!
> When they give him the sack, they'll take him back,
>   Sit down! Sit down!
> When the speedup comes, just twiddle your thumbs,
>   Sit down! Sit down!
> When the boss won't talk, don't take a walk,
>   Sit down! Sit down!
>   from a song written by Maurice Sugar,
>   a UAW attorney

The strike that gave the letters C I O an electric quality took place at General Motors in late December 1936 and early 1937. As noted, it changed the character of the American labor movement. It also led to a significant improvement in the standard of living of millions of workers—an improvement we still enjoy today.

The horseless carriage of the twentieth century was in many ways like the iron horse of the nineteenth. By the 1930s, the automobile industry had become the crucial center of American manufacture. A $4 billion industry—producing cars, trucks, taxicabs, hearses, buses, and tractors—its origin went back to pre–Civil War days when a gasoline engine was displayed in Europe.

No one paid much attention to this toy until the 1880s, when Gottlieb Daimler of Germany built a single-cylinder combustion machine. A decade later, the novelty spread to America, where dozens of mechanics and promoters engaged in a mad race to place their models on the street first. Among them were Henry Ford and William C. Durant. By 1913 there were five dozen companies in the field, producing such models as the Oldsmobile, Ford, Maxwell, Reo, Cadillac, Studebaker, and Packard. In 1914 Ford alone sold 248,000 cars, compared to 10,607 five years before. Its profit was a very respectable $30.3 million.

Henry Ford, born in Dearborn, Michigan, in 1863, was a semi-literate and bigoted man. (He had never heard of Benedict Arnold, couldn't define the word *commenced* during a 1919 libel suit, and was an anti-Semite who later accepted an Iron Cross from Hitler.) But he knew automobiles, and he appreciated the value of a mass market. The early Tin Lizzie (Model T) brought him wealth and power. In 1914 he put into effect a $5-a-day wage in order to guarantee a stable labor force. It was a fabulous sum at the time and gained him the reputation of a benefactor.

William C. Durant's position, on the other hand, was that of a promoter. He invented no cars, but he was skilled at exchanging stocks and grouping individual companies into empires. In 1885 he joined with a Flint, Michigan, insurance salesman to sell two-wheel carts to farm-implement firms. The carts were immensely popular. A millionaire at forty, Durant turned to the horseless carriage. He picked up the small, almost bankrupt Buick Manufacturing Company. With the help of technical geniuses such as Charles Mott, an axle maker, and Albert Champion, one of the great names in spark plugs, he converted Buick into a leading auto firm.

Then, using Buick as a base, Durant turned to a wild promotion of mergers. By exchanging stock with various firms, he was able in 1908–1909 to amalgamate Buick, Cadillac, Oldsmobile, Oakland, ten auto-parts makers, three truck companies, and five smaller auto manufacturers into the General Motors Company.

Bankers forced Durant to step aside as head of GM in 1910, replacing him with Charles Nash and, later, Walter P. Chrysler. But in 1911, Durant secured the services of a fabulous Swiss mechanic, Louis Chevrolet, and began to produce a low-cost car, which he named after his mechanic. Before long, the Chevrolet company, with the help of Pierre Du Pont and John J. Raskob, bought out the General Motors Company.

The trend toward empire building in the auto industry ran parallel to amazing advances in the mechanization of labor, such as the conveyor and assembly line. Giant factories burgeoned with thousands of workers in a single oblong structure. Another result of mechanization was the stopwatch time study, in which fractions of a second became important and laborers paced themselves to electric machines.

The auto industry was the very incarnation of mass production. Frederick W. Taylor, the father of scientific management, had predicted that mass production would lead to not only a higher yield of goods but also greater harmony between labor and capital. With vastly increased profits, the companies could pay more—and thus satisfy their workers.

But Taylor was wrong. Car manufacturers, like the railroad owners, were in no mood to share their wealth with their workers or make life easier for them. Their aim was simply to make a profit. Mass production led to speedup. Employers increased the speed of the machine, forcing employees to keep pace.

Workers subjected to speedup came home too tired to do anything but eat and sleep. They grew old before their time. Many had what was called the shakes, a constant nervous twitch. "It takes your guts out, that line," was the comment of one worker. "During the past two decades," Herbert Harris wrote in the 1930s, "the industry's emphasis on youth, with its greater speed and endurance, has kept displacing older employees at an ever accelerating rate."

In the light of such conditions, unionism should have swept the auto plants early in their history, particularly since there were already 127,000 men and women employed in the industry as of 1907, and 377,000 a decade later. In 1901, the AFL granted jurisdiction in this field to the Carriage and Wagon Workers' Union. But when that union refused to surrender jurisdiction over carpenters, electricians, patternmakers, and a host of others to craft unions at the 1913 AFL convention, it was expelled.

Early on, the Wobblies tried to unionize the Ford Highland Park plant but were frustrated when Ford introduced the $5-a-day wage. With 10,000 people waiting in line for those jobs, few workers were disposed to join the IWW. The AFL made another feeble effort to organize the industry in 1926, but gave up when General Motors and Ford refused to help in the drive.

By 1933 many auto workers, however, were ready to try again. The number of employees in the plants had shrunk during the last four years, and wages had come down. An independent union of skilled workers, the Mechanics Educational Society, struck many shops in protest against the reduction of average wages. The following year came the Toledo Auto-Lite strike and a campaign by the AFL, which enrolled 210,000 men and women. The trouble was that the old federation was not clear as to whether these workers would be kept together in a single industrial union or divided up among the existing craft unions.

Meanwhile, the corporations began forming company unions and forcing their employees to join them or lose their jobs.

Another obstacle to union organization was the hiring of company spies. At Ford, a former prizefighter named Harry Bennett headed a special "service department." At its core were a few hundred thugs who physically attacked suspected unionists. In addition, thousands of ordinary workers were paid a few pennies an hour to spy on their fellow workers.

Chrysler and General Motors preferred to have their spying done by outside detective agencies. General Motors spent almost a million dollars for this purpose in the two-and-a-half years ending July 31, 1936. A Pinkerton spokesperson boasted to Senator Robert M. LaFollette, Jr., that his spies had burrowed so deeply into the union structure that one had become vice president of a national union, fourteen had become presidents of local unions, and thirty-eight were local secretaries. As a result of La-Follette's hearings, Congress passed laws making industrial espionage illegal. In the meantime, spy activities hampered labor's efforts. By August 1935, AFL membership in the auto plants was down to a paltry 20,000.

The formation of the CIO gave auto workers a new shot in the arm. The recently formed United Auto Workers was affiliated with the CIO and gained recruits by leaps and bounds. A number of quickie strikes in Cleveland, Toledo, and Flint were successful, giving the campaign additional impetus.

Then in November 1936, four workers at the General Motors plant in Atlanta were discharged for wearing union buttons and protesting a 20 percent wage cut. That was the spark that ignited the bonfire. The Atlanta workers decided to strike. But instead of walking out of the plant and forming picket lines, they used a novel tactic—the sitdown. The Wobblies had staged a sitdown at a General Electric plant in 1906. Italian workers had sat inside their factories in 1919, hoping to take over the government. At Pecs, Hungary, in 1934, coal miners stayed down in the mines and threatened to commit suicide rather than accept prevailing working conditions. From 1935 to 1937, there were nine hundred sitdowns in the United States, most of them successful.

Employers called the sitdown illegal, but illegal or not, the advantages for strikers were obvious. An outside picket line could easily be attacked by police, troops, or professional strikebreakers. Employers would think twice, however, before sending strikebreakers to fight inside a plant, where valuable machinery might be destroyed.

The Atlanta sitdown strike just happened. No CIO leader planned it. Evidently the workers asked themselves why they should picket on the outside and get their heads busted, when they were fairly safe sitting inside. A few weeks after the Atlanta sitdown, the idea spread to a GM plant in Kansas City after another worker was fired.

At this point, the CIO asked General Motors for a meeting to iron out grievances, but the company refused. In late December the sitdown spread to two of the GM body plants in Cleveland.

It began over a trivial matter—the company's postponement of a meeting to discuss wage cuts. But for seven thousand workers, that was the last straw.

Two days after the strike began, it spread to Flint. Workers became aware that the company was moving dies out of the Fisher One plant, evidently intending to ship them to other shops where labor relations were not so turbulent. That was the signal for Bob Travis, Roy Reuther, and other young leaders of the UAW to seize the plant. Plans had been under way for some time to strike the GM empire; the movement of dies sped it up. Three thousand workers took over the factory with no difficulty. Neither the plant police nor anyone else dared interfere.

Organizing the forty-four-day sitdown at Flint was a complicated matter. The five hundred to one thousand men holed up at Fisher One (women were sent home) had to be fed and given opportunities for relaxation. Workers were divided into "families" of fifteen, each headed by a captain, each finding a nook in which to sleep—within unfinished car bodies or on car-cushion wadding placed on the floor. Each man was required to shower daily. For diversion there were Ping-Pong, cards, checkers, books, magazines, labor classes, and even boxing. The sitdowners were very careful that no company property was damaged.

As the union had anticipated, the strikes at Flint and Cleveland progressively forced a shutdown of other GM operations—at Delco-Remy, AC Sparkplug, Buick, and Chevrolet assembly lines. And the sitdown continued to spread further.

Stung, the giant automaker struck back quickly with time-tested methods. Three days after the sitdown began, company attorneys secured an injunction, from a judge who owned 3,365 shares of GM stock, ordering strikers out of the plant. The sheriff was unable to serve the papers. His "Clear out of here . . . or else" threat was ignored. Normally in a situation like that, the company would have appealed to the governor or president for troops; but in the climate of the 1930s, such an appeal was not as automatic as it had been in previous years.

The next effort to break the strike was an attempt by police to

Sleeping quarters of auto workers in a Fisher Body plant during the historic sitdown strike of 1937   INTERNATIONAL UNION, UNITED AUTO WORKERS

evict strikers at another plant to which the sitdown had spread: Fisher Two. The eviction plan was simple: First, deny heat and food to the strikers; then, make a direct physical siege.

GM had provided heat in the first days of the sitdown. But on January 11, 1937, with the temperature at 16 degrees and due to fall, the company shut off the heat. A few hours later, union supporters carrying the evening dinner to the sitdowners were denied entry to the plant by GM guards who remained inside. Hundreds of workers from other auto plants hurried to the scene, and soon the most famous skirmish in CIO history—the Battle of Bulls' Run—ensued. Strikers inside, armed with billy clubs they themselves had manufactured, attacked the guards and broke the locks on the gate. The guards retreated to the women's washroom; deputies and police tried to rescue them.

For the next five hours, there was a state of bedlam. One of the union leaders, Vic Reuther (another of the three Reuther brothers), cried out, "Pickets, back to your posts! Men in the plant, get your fire hoses going!" As police tossed tear gas into the plant and at the pickets, the strikers inside began hosing the police. Other strikers inside and out threw two-pound automobile door hinges at the police. The skirmish ended in a few minutes when the officers, their uniforms freezing on their bodies, retreated.

Around 9 P.M., half of Flint's police force, about fifty men, arrived for the second assault. Reuther shouted, "We want peace; General Motors chose war. Give it to them." The strikers rocked the sheriff's auto back and forth and overturned it—with the sheriff and some of his deputies still in it. It was all the sheriff could do to get out of the vehicle. Three other police cars were seized by the pickets. From the roof of the factory, sitdowners with homemade slingshots heaved hinges at the beleaguered police. The outside pickets formed a barricade of automobiles between themselves and the police, then hurled nuts, bolts, empty bottles, and other missiles at them. The police never made it to the plant. They were pushed back to a bridge 150 feet away.

At this point, enraged police, disregarding orders by their superiors, reached for their guns and began shooting. The battle now took on a more serious turn. A sitdowner on the roof cried out, "I've been hit," and there were other similar cries. Strike leader Bob Travis was carried off to the hospital with gas burns from a tear-gas grenade.

Fourteen union people were wounded; thirty-six police were sent to the hospital. At midnight, five hours after the fighting had started, the police withdrew and the Battle of Bulls' Run was over.

At the union office the next morning, organizers were besieged by workers from other GM plants who wanted to join the UAW. And ten thousand more unionists, many from out of town, gath-

Troops stand guard outside an auto plant during the Flint, Michigan, sitdown strike, 1937. INTERNATIONAL UNION, UNITED AUTO WORKERS

ered for an anticipated showdown. The governor brought together representatives of the CIO and the company in the hopes of effecting a compromise—but in vain.

Then on January 17, it became known that GM was to begin negotiations with another so-called union, one of its own making —the Flint Alliance. It would recognize two unions. The sitdowners, about to evacuate their factories, decided to stay in. A few days later, as morale began to sag among UAW members in Flint and elsewhere, the union executed a new coup. It seized another big plant in Flint: Chevy Four.

In response, Governor Frank Murphy sent twelve hundred troops to the scene; heat and light were cut off. But the third

Reuther brother, Walter, threatened to start bonfires in the plant to keep warm. It was a bleak moment, when anything could happen. Five thousand pickets, armed with pipes, clubs, and crowbars, were gathered outside Fisher One. An injunction against the strikers again was ignored; so was a threat to impose a $15 million fine on the union.

In this tense situation, the company finally backed off. It agreed to negotiate with CIO president John L. Lewis. Weekly production of GM cars was down to a mere 1,500 (compared with 28,825 at Ford and 25,350 at Chrysler). The company agreed to recognize the UAW at the seventeen plants then on strike, to drop lawsuits, to take no reprisals against the strikers, and not to interfere with workers joining the UAW. The agreement was to run for six months.

It was by no means the victory the union wanted. In particular, the word *sole* was left out of collective bargaining rights, so that the company was not limited to bargaining solely with the UAW. It was legally free to deal with other unions as well, if it wanted to. But in practice there was no stopping the UAW at this point. In the wake of the big strike, there were eighteen more individual sitdowns in GM plants within twenty days. A few months later, 59,000 Chrysler workers occupied their factories in Detroit. In the month after the GM strike, there were 247 sitdowns involving 193,000 workers.

On March 2, 1937, almost two months after the Battle of Bulls' Run, U.S. Steel announced it was granting bargaining rights to the Steel Workers Organizing Committee, raising wages 10 percent, and reducing the work week to 40 hours. Rather than face the prospect of sitdowns, the big steel company, controlled by J. P. Morgan, agreed to bargain with John L. Lewis and his assistant Philip Murray. Within three months, 140 other companies followed the lead of U.S. Steel and signed pacts with the CIO steel union. Some held out—notably Bethlehem, Republic, and Youngstown. But the heart of the industry was now unionized.

The *Newark Evening News* takes a critical view of labor leader John L. Lewis in this cartoon drawn by Lute Pease, entitled How Does He Do It?   LIBRARY OF CONGRESS

The sitdown tactic had finally done what had been impossible for decades—unionized the core of America's mass production industries.

12 A New Era?

An Injury to One Is the Concern of All.
   slogan of the Knights of Labor
   in the 1880s, still used frequently
   in the labor movement today

Toiling millions now are waking—
See them marching on.
All the tyrants now are shaking
Ere their power's gone.

Storm the fort, ye Knights of Labor
Battle for your cause:
Equal rights for every neighbor
Down with tyrant laws.
            a Knights of Labor song

Not all was love and harmony between labor and capital in the decades after the 1936–38 strike wave. There were many years in which the number of strikes was even greater than in 1937. From 1940 through 1955 alone, there were 65,000 work stoppages.

Even the liberal president, Franklin Roosevelt, tried his hand at strikebreaking occasionally. In June 1941, Roosevelt sent thirty-five hundred troops to seize the plant of the North American Aviation Company at Inglewood, California. The strike of 12,000 United Auto Worker members was effectively smashed by this action.

Periodically too, one still read items such as this one from *The New York Times* of September 8, 1953: "HYDEN, KY. Sept. 7— In the capital of this nonunion producing country here, John L. Lewis's United Mine Workers union has been waging a campaign for more than two years to bring the operators under contract. Eight organizers have been shot; one of them died, another is completely paralyzed. Cars have been dynamited and union meetings, members' homes, and friendly merchants' stores have been blasted or fired upon."

Strikebreaking and union busting did not become extinct by any means. The strike of Local 833 UAW against the Kohler Company of Kohler, Wisconsin, which began in April 1954, lasted for eight years.

But there were also many major strikes in which the contending sides seemed almost like friends. For ten weeks in 1970, for instance, the largest industrial corporation in the United States, General Motors, confronted the largest industrial union in the United States, the United Auto Workers. Four hundred thousand UAW members were on strike, a few of them veterans of the Battle of Bulls' Run and other strikes of the 1930s.

But this time there were no strikebreakers, no scabs, no Pinkertons, no shootings, teargassing, clubbings—and no arrests. The union did not organize flying squadrons, and its members picketed only to be eligible for strike benefits, not to fight strikebreakers. There was no fear of attack by the police or National Guard, and small likelihood that management would seek injunctions in courts. The most powerful weapon of the union this time was a strike fund, upward of $100 million, out of which weekly benefits were paid for those on the picket line.

Following the 1936–38 strike wave, employers did not automatically embrace unionism. They fought it hammer and tongs in many industries—the textile industry, for example—and in some areas—the South, for instance. But where labor had illustrated its power, relations with management entered a new era: not of peace but of greater accommodation.

World War II was also a major factor in changing the character of labor relations. Four years after the Little Steel strike and the shooting of ten workers on Memorial Day 1937, the National Labor Relations Board (NLRB) ordered the four companies to reinstate all the employees they had fired in 1937 and bargain with the steel union. By then the United States was preparing for war, and companies like Bethlehem and Republic were receiving immense government contracts to produce steel for the impending war effort. If they had refused to obey the NLRB order, they would have lost lucrative contracts.

The same kind of pressure convinced the Ford Motor Company to come to terms with the UAW after a short strike in April 1941. The $123 million federal contract for aviation engines given the company a few months before undoubtedly was an important factor in Ford's decision.

The government spent $288 billion for World War II. It insisted that unions and employers agree to labor peace so that war material could be produced without interruption. The unions (except for John L. Lewis's miners) all pledged not to strike during hostilities, and a War Labor Board (WLB) was established to settle disputes. It had the power of issuing binding decisions.

The War Labor Board was the ultimate arbiter between labor and capital, and tended to compromise the disputes between them. Against the wishes of the unions for a closed shop and of the employers for an open shop, for instance, the WLB granted the unions maintenance of membership. That meant that a worker was free to join or not to join a union; but once he had joined, he was required to maintain his membership.

On the issue of wages, the WLB proclaimed a Little Steel formula, restricting raises for all workers to a total of 15 percent. Unions felt they were shortchanged because prices went up much more than that.

Perhaps if the war hadn't intervened, employers might have mounted a campaign to break the militant unions formed in the 1930s. But not only would such a campaign have been illegal, it would have been self-defeating. Bethlehem, for instance, had $1 billion in war contracts, all certain of showing big profits. Why jeopardize that bonanza?

Unions too might grumble about the fact that WLB decisions were unfavorable. Wages tended to lag behind increases in prices.

But the WLB decision on maintenance of membership helped add 6 million members to union ranks from 1940 to 1945. By 1945 there were 13 million members in the AFL and CIO, and 2 million more in independent unions—a total of 15 million, or five times the total membership in 1933.

In the years after the sitdowns, employers found other means of containing unions besides open strikebreaking. One of them was the back door contract. Many employers decided it was better to deal with moderate AFL unions than face more militant CIO unions. They signed agreements behind the backs of their employees, without giving them an opportunity to choose which union they wanted.

The Kaiser company in Portland, Oregon, for instance, came to terms with Local 72 of the Boilermakers which ultimately required 65,000 workers to join that union. At the time the pact was signed, however, only a skeleton crew of 500 was employed by the company. Thus, before they could express their choice through a vote, 64,500 future employees were required to join the AFL rather than the CIO.

In Chicago, supermarket and grocery companies signed a back door contract with an AFL union for 10,000 workers, even though the union had not a single member at the time. Dave Beck of the teamsters' union added thousands of members to his union on the West Coast because employers preferred to deal with him rather than the CIO's Harry Bridges. Back door contracts involved hundreds of thousands of workers. Under those agreements, relations between labor and management were cozy rather than militant. There were few strikes and thus no need for employers to smash them.

Once hostilities were over in 1945 and the no-strike pledge was no longer in force, there was an eruption of strikes. There usually is after a war. General Motors' workers in ninety-two factories went out for 113 days. National walkouts occurred in steel, coal,

Strikers march through Carnegie, Pennsylvania, during the Big Steel strike of 1946.   UNITED STEELWORKERS OF AMERICA

and electric products industries, in maritime organizations, and on the railroads. City-wide strikes paralyzed Stamford, Lancaster, Oakland, Rochester, Houston, Hartford, and Camden.

But there was no life-and-death character to those strikes, no attempt to call in strikebreakers or smash unions. *Fortune* magazine wrote that "the strikes and strike threats of 1945–46 generated violent emotions, but it was an impressive fact that for the first time a great wave of strikes stirred up almost no physical violence."

That first postwar wave ended in a general wage increase of 18½ cents an hour for most mass-production workers. The fol-

A member of the CIO Packinghouse Workers walks through a Chicago railroad car to win support from riders during a 1948 strike.   GEORGE MEANY MEMORIAL ARCHIVES/AFL-CIO

lowing year, the raise was 15 cents. In addition, many new ideas were introduced into collective bargaining, all of them giving millions of organized workers more security.

In 1948, Walter Reuther, president of the United Auto Workers, negotiated a novel contract with the auto firms. Under the new pact, auto workers received two kinds of raises—annual raises and escalator raises based on the cost of living. When the cost of living rose, wages went up; when it fell (very infrequently), they went down. Soon the same provisions went into thousands of other union contracts.

Another feature of postwar bargaining was the inclusion of

Pickets seeking pensions and other fringe benefits slow down cars on a highway near an aircraft plant to discourage people from entering the plant.   GEORGE MEANY MEMORIAL ARCHIVES / AFL-CIO

many more fringe benefits. Up to then, unions concentrated primarily on getting wages raised. Now labor began to bargain for paid holidays, paid vacations, health and welfare plans, pensions, and supplemental unemployment benefits (over and above what the government paid).

Other factors led to the accommodation between established unions and corporations. Union leaders became less militant, seeking security for themselves as well as their members. Whereas a CIO union official's term of office had formerly been a year, it went up to two, three, or more years. Contracts that had been signed for a year were now for two, three, or even five years. Employers were willing to bend a little to get long-term contracts, which assured them a stable labor force for a number of years.

Steelworkers point in the opposite direction from the employment office.

Most of all, the country was enormously prosperous in the postwar period. The rest of the Western world had been badly battered by a war that took 52 million lives and destroyed at least $1 trillion in property. But the United States was untouched by bombs. Its factories were intact, capable of producing twice as many heavy industrial goods as before the war. There was a large market for American products both abroad and at home. People had been waiting five or six years to buy a new car or a new home. Any boost in wages, moreover, could usually be passed on to consumers in the form of higher prices.

While employers still fought to keep wages and benefits as low as possible, there was a greater tendency to come to terms. Moreover, whatever wage increase was won by General Motors and U.S. Steel workers was almost automatically granted by lesser corporations and accepted by the unions.

A measure of moderation between labor and capital was the pattern for twenty-five years after the war. That pattern didn't apply to poorly organized industries or to certain antiunion areas. There, employers found other means to hobble unions. Under the Wagner Act passed during the New Deal, a union could gain recognition without striking simply by winning a majority in an election conducted by the National Labor Relations Board. The NLRB also was charged with defending a worker's right to join a union. If an employee was discharged for union activity, the NLRB could order reinstatement with back pay.

That was all to the good of course, but little by little the NLRB turned more conservative. It became much harder to win reinstatement for a discharged worker; many cases went to court, where they languished for a long time. Thus a company could fire ten or fifteen leaders of a union organizing drive, scaring off everyone else, and often pay no penalty. By the time the NLRB might order reinstatement, and by the time the order went through the courts several years later, the other workers would have lost interest in the union drive. Year by year, therefore, the percentage of NLRB elections won by unions kept falling; by the 1980s it was less than half. Only a few new groups were unionized—teachers, government workers, service employees, and one or two others.

As for collective bargaining negotiations for wages, hours, and the like, employers found that they did not have to resort to strikebreakers and violence as often as in the past. Since it was a generally prosperous period, they could compromise with a union and pass on the cost of wage increases to the consumer. Or they could wait out a union, hoping its members would give in as they missed one paycheck after another.

That was the general attitude until the late 1970s. By then the United States was no longer in the same favorable condition it had been in after World War II. It was losing ground competitively to Germany, Japan, and other nations. Its steel industry was in severe decline; its auto industry was under pressure from Japanese auto firms. Some of that was compensated for by the growth of new high technology industries, such as the computer industry. But from 1979 to 1983, the country experienced two severe recessions—worse than any since the 1930s. At one point unemployment reached a rate of 10 percent. More than 10 million workers were seeking jobs; a few million more had given up hope of finding work and stopped looking.

Under those circumstances, employers began to demand concessions from unions. They asked that benefits gained in previous years be given up. At first unions resisted. In 1978, steelworkers at three plants struck, refusing to give back previous gains. In 1979, Westinghouse workers "hit the bricks" for seven weeks, rather than relinquish what they had once won. Caterpillar Tractor was struck for eleven weeks; International Harvester, almost a half year. In all those instances, the unions won.

But beginning in 1979, the near bankrupt Chrysler Corporation demanded one concession after another from UAW members. Workers, fearful that their jobs would be lost, agreed to cut their pay by $46 a week and gave up other benefits. Altogether, the cuts left them $3 an hour behind workers at General Motors.

The concessions movement became a stampede—and it continued even when recovery set in during 1983–84. Not only near bankrupt companies but profitable ones forced unions to give back gains they had won over the years. With millions of unemployed breathing down their necks, ready to take their jobs if they went on strike, many workers preferred to yield some of their benefits rather than lose their jobs.

The list of corporations and industries that exacted concessions from their employees reads like a who's who of big business—General Motors, Ford, the whole steel industry, the airlines, International Harvester, Caterpillar Tractor, most of the aluminum industry, many construction firms, meat-packers, glass companies, newspapers, railroads, rubber companies, trucking firms. A number of corporations declared bankruptcy, even though they were still solvent, in order to cancel union contracts. That was a new tactic, with grave implications.

As the nation entered a period of recovery in 1983, there were signs of union resistance. Here and there, a labor-management conflict took on the appearance of the old labor wars—not as bitter or as violent, but with unsettling resemblances.

On July 1, 1983, copper miners in Arizona went on strike against the Phelps Dodge Corporation when it refused to meet the terms agreed to by other copper corporations. Thirteen unions collaborated in that walkout.

A month after the stoppage began, Governor Bruce Babbitt, a Democrat, dispatched almost a thousand state police and National Guardsmen to the towns of Clifton and Morenci to defend strikebreakers being hired by the company. Along with the troops, the governor sent in armored personnel carriers, helicopters, SWAT (Special Weapons and Tactics) teams with M-16 rifles, and snipers armed with high-powered guns.

In the town of Ajo, two hundred miles away, where 325 miners were on strike, a similar scene was enacted. On August 27, according to the strikers, state police surrounded and invaded strikers' homes, arresting 40 people without warrants.

Officers of the Arizona Department of Public Safety fire tear gas on copper miners who had gathered on the first anniversary of their strike against the Phelps Dodge Corporation.   AP/WIDE WORLD PHOTOS

The strike at Phelps Dodge was still under way in 1984, with no settlement in sight. Like so many other mining confrontations in the nineteenth and early twentieth centuries, it was a slow fuse that could ignite at any moment.

Another sign of the times was the strike of 12,700 Greyhound bus drivers and associated workers, which began on November 3, 1983. The company was demanding concessions that would have reduced wages and benefits by about 25 percent. The employees were bitter about the demand of concessions because Greyhound had earned $19 million the previous year; and its parent company, $103 million. Management argued, however, that it needed more money to fight off the competition of other bus companies and airlines. In the end, Greyhound employees accepted a 7.8 percent cut in pay and the loss of other benefits, totaling 13 to 15 percent.

In those and other instances, one could detect again the ingredients of new class wars. Tempers were growing short, particularly since the nation was enjoying a modest economic recovery.

Is America primed to return to the "good old days"? Will we witness again an era of widespread and violent strikebreaking, the use of troops and injunctions, the killing of scores of strikers?

Or will adversity pull together the union movement for new campaigns like those of the 1890s and 1930s? Will labor find a new method to defend its hopes for a better life—for instance, through politics?

No one can say in advance. All one can do is point out that the union movement has tended to change its shape and form in accordance with changes in the American enterprise system. There were no unions at all in Colonial days, before the capitalist system began to take shape. Then after the Revolution and until the Civil War, unions were weak and tenuous, just like the economic system. A relatively small but stable union movement appeared during the 1880s and continued until the Great Depression; its leaders took on some of the character of the business world it challenged. That was the era of simple or business unionism. After the Great Depression, America itself changed drastically: The government, which was supposed to leave the economy alone, now played a big role in shaping economic destiny. A new labor movement, based on the industrial form and with greater social concern than that of the old AFL, appeared to match this change.

The American system is again changing drastically. This is now the era of the conglomerate and multinational corporation, and the era of massive government intervention in the daily life of the economy. If the government raises interest rates, housing sales go down and thousands of workers lose their jobs. If the president appoints conservatives to the National Labor Relations Board, as Ronald Reagan did, the unions find it more difficult to attract new members.

This is the reality that the labor movement will be adjusting to in the coming years. Just exactly how labor will react remains to be seen, but it will certainly be in a different way than at present.

FURTHER READING

Austin, Aleine. *The Labor Story*. New York: Coward-McCann, 1949.

Bornstein, Jerry. *Unions in Transition*. New York: Julian Messner, 1981.

Brecher, Jeremy. *Strike!* Sun Valley, Idaho: Straight Arrow Books, 1972. Paper edition: Boston: South End Press, 1977.

Fine, Sidney. *Sit-Down: The General Motors Strike of 1936–37*. Ann Arbor, Michigan: University of Michigan Press, 1969.

Fisher, Leonard E. *The Unions*. New York: Holiday House, 1982.

Flagler, John J. *Modern Trade Unionism*. Minneapolis: Lerner Publications, 1970.

Gardner, Joseph L. *Labor on the March: The Story of America's Unions*. New York: American Heritage Publishing Co., 1969.

Gilchrist, Cherry. *People at Work: Nineteen Thirty to the Nineteen Eighty's*. North Pomfret, Vermont: David & Charles, 1983.

Harris, Janet. *Thursday's Daughters: The Story of Women Working in America.* New York: Harper & Row, 1977.

Haskins, Jim. *The Long Struggle: The Story of American Labor.* Philadelphia: Westminster, 1976.

Kornbluh, Joyce L. *Rebel Voices.* Ann Arbor, Michigan: University of Michigan Press, 1964. Paper edition: 1968.

Kraus, Henry. *The Many and the Few.* Los Angeles: Plantin Press, 1947.

Levinson, Edward. *Labor on the March.* New York: Harper & Row, 1938.

Levy, Elizabeth, and Richards, Tad. *Struggle and Lose, Struggle and Win: The United Mine Workers.* New York: Four Winds Press, 1977.

Lindsey, Almont. *The Pullman Strike.* Chicago: University of Chicago Press, 1942. Paper edition: 1964.

Matthiessen, Peter. *Sal Si Puedes: Cesar Chavez and the New American Revolution.* New York: Random House, 1969.

Pelling, Henry. *American Labor.* Chicago: University of Chicago Press, 1960.

Schwartz, Alvin. *The Unions.* New York: Viking, 1972.

Selden, Bernice. *The Mill Girls: Lucy Larcom, Harriet Hanson Robinson & Sarah G. Bagley.* New York: Atheneum, 1983.

Selvin, David F. *Champions of Labor.* New York: Abelard-Schuman, 1967.

Vorse, Mary Heaton. *Labor's New Millions.* Reprint of 1938 edition. Salem, New Hampshire: Ayer Co., 1969.

Werstein, Irving. *Pie in the Sky: An American Struggle. The Wobblies and Their Times.* New York: Delacorte, 1969.

Yellen, Samuel. *American Labor Struggles.* Reprint of 1936 edition. Salem, New Hampshire: Ayer Co., 1969.

INDEX

Page numbers in *italics* refer to captions.

democracy, 15, 29
  labor disputes and, 6–8
Democratic party, U.S., 28, 69
Democratic-Republican party,
  U.S., 19
depressions, 14, 15, 20, 21, 83,
  126
  of 1873, 14, 38, 39, 51, 52
  of 1893, 66–67
  of 1920–21, 121
Diamond Special, 72
Du Pont, Pierre, 135
Durant, William C., 134–135
Dynamite (Adamic), 46

Erie Railroad, 47, 56, 59
Ettor, Joseph J. "Smiling Joe,"
  99–100, 102, 103, 107
Ettor-Giovannitti Defense
  Committee, 107
Evans, Oliver, 49
Everett Cotton Mill, 98

farmers, 10–11, 48, 50
Federal Aviation
  Administration (FAA),
  25–31
Federalist party, U.S., 18–20
Federal Labor Relations
  Authority, 30
Federal Mediation Commission,
  112–113
Federal Society of Journeymen
  Cordwainers, 16–20
fire fighters, strikes of, 3
Fisk, Jim, 47
Fitch, James, 13
Fitzpatrick, John, 112–113,
  114, 118, 120
Flint Alliance, 142
Flint sitdown strike, 138–141
Ford, Henry, 109, 134, 136

Ford Motor Company, 134,
  136, 142, 146, 154
Fortune, 148
Foss, Eugene N., 102
Foster, William Z., 111–118,
  120
*Frank Leslie's Illustrated
  Newspaper,* 85
Frick, Henry Clay, 65
fringe benefits, 150

Garfield, James A., 48
garment industry, 93–96,
  126–127
Garrett, John W., 51
Gary, Elbert Henry, 113,
  114–115, 116, 117, 118,
  120
Geisenheimer, Frederick W.,
  33
General Electric, 110, 137
General Managers' Association
  (GMA), 72–73, 74, 78, 79
General Motors Corporation
  (GM), 136, 152, 153, 154
  establishment of, 134
  strikes against, 131, 133,
  135–142, *139, 141,* 147
German Americans, 59
Gilded Age, 46–49
Giovannitti, Arturo, 100, 103,
  107
Golden Twenties, 121–126
Gompers, Samuel, 81–83, *82,*
  99, 112, 116
Gorman, Francis J., 127–128
Gould, Jay, 37, 47
government employees, strikes
  of, 3, 22–31
Gowen, Franklin Benjamin,
  37–44, 51
Grace, Eugene, 125

National Conference of
    Charities and Correction,
    101
National Cordage Company,
    66
National Guard, 1, 3, 55, *55*,
    57, 65, 76–77, 119, 129,
    130
National Industrial Union of
    Textile Workers, 102
National Labor Relations Act
    (Wagner Act), 22–23, 152
National Labor Relations
    Board (NLRB), 23, 30,
    89, 145–146, 152–153, 156
National Labor Union, 80
National Recovery
    Administration (NRA),
    127
National Trades' Union, 21
Newark Evening News, 143
New Deal, 126–127
New York Central Railroad,
    47, 49, 52, 59
New York *Sun,* 64, 100
New York Times, 72, 101, 102,
    144–145
New York *Tribune,* 32, 54
New York Typographical
    Society, 15
New York *World,* 45, 59
North American Aviation
    Company, 144

O'Donnell, Charles, 43
Olney, Richard B., 73–74
open shop, 125
Open Shop Association, 125
Outlook, 32

Palmer, A. Mitchell, 119
Parks, Sam, 87

Parsons, Albert, 59, 60
Pease, Lute, *143*
Pennsylvania Coal Company,
    95
Pennsylvania Constitution, 19
Pennsylvania Railroad, 49, 52,
    56–59
Pennsylvania's Day With the
    Rope, 44–45
Phelps Dodge strike, 154–155,
    155
Philadelphia and Reading
    Railroad (Reading
    Railroad), 37, 38–39
Philadelphia *Times,* 45
Philadelphia Typographical
    Society, 15
pickets, 9, 10, 27, 100,
    101–102, 103, 128, 137,
    150
Pinkerton, Allan, 39, 40
Pinkerton Detective Agency,
    35, 39, 40, 41, 64, 65, 101,
    136
Pittsburgh, Pa., railroad strike
    in, 56–59
Pittsburgh Coal Company,
    124
Poli, Robert E., 26
police, 138–140
    in Lawrence strike, 101–102
    in steel strike of 1919,
        116–117
    strikes of, 3
Pressed Steel Car plant, 111
printers' strikes, 15
Professional Air Traffic
    Controllers Organization
    (PATCO), 9, 25–31
    strike of, 26, 28–31, *29*
Progressive Era, 92–95
Proletario, Il, 100

steel strikes, *continued*
  (1946), *148*
  (1956), 1, 2–3
Steel Workers Organizing
  Committee, 142
Steffens, Lincoln, 92
Stephenson, George, 49
Stevens, John, 49
stock market crash, 126
Stockyard Labor Council,
  112–113
Stolberg, Benjamin, 127
stretch-out, 127
Strike Commission, U.S., 74
strikes:
  aim of, 8
  attitudes and opinions about,
    3
  Big Steel, *148*
  carpenters', 15, 21
  Caterpillar Tractor, 153
  coal miners', 35–36, 37, 38,
    39–43
  Coeur d'Alene, 65
  cordwainers', 16–20
  cost of, 6, *6*, 32–33
  Cripple Creek, 93
  first, 15
  General Motors, 131, 133,
    135–142, *139, 141,* 147
  in Golden Twenties,
    122–124
  Greyhound, 155
  Homestead, 64–65, *65, 66,*
    67
  as illegal conspiracy, 10,
    16–21, 22
  illegal vs. legal, 3–4, 24
  inconvenience of, 5
  International Harvester,
    153
  Lawrence textile, 97–107
  letter carriers', 24

strikes, *continued*
  Little Steel, 1–2, *2,* 145
  longshoremen's, 128–129
  Minneapolis, 130–131
  negotiations before, 8
  in 1970s, 153
  origin of, 1–15
  Phelps Dodge, 154–155, *155*
  Pressed Steel Car plant, 111
  Professional Air Traffic
    Controllers', 26, 28–31, *29*
  Pullman, 72–79
  questions about, 3–5
  railroad, 32, 49, 52–62, *54,*
    55, 60, 65–66, 68, 69,
    70–79
  right to call, 86, 87
  shipyard, 6
  shirtwaist workers', 95
  simple unionist view of, 82
  sitdown, 110–111, 137–143
  steel, 1–3, *2,* 64–65, *65, 66,*
    67, 113–120, *148*
  streetcar, 64
  successful vs. unsuccessful,
    84
  textile workers', 21, 51–52,
    97–107, *105,* 127–128
  Toledo, 129–130, *130,* 136
  voting on, 5, 9
  Westinghouse, 153
  wildcat, letter carriers', 24
  after World War II,
    147–148, *148*
sweatshops, 93
Sweetser, E. LeRoy, 103
Swift, Gustavus, 109, 110
Sylvis, William H., 80–81

Taft, Mrs. William Howard,
  104
Tarbell, Ida, 92
Taylor, Frederick W., 135

Taylor, George W., 8
teachers' strikes, 3–4, 24
Teamsters' Local 574, 131
teamsters' union, 88, 131
technological advances, 109
Teoli, Camella, 105
textile industry, 145
    strikes in, 21, 51–52, 97–107,
        105, 127–128
Thornton, John, 25, 27
Toledo, Ohio, auto workers'
    strike in, 129–130, *130*,
    136
Toomey, John A., 117
totalitarianism, labor disputes
    and, 6, 8
Trainmen's Union, 52–53
Travis, Bob, 138, 140
Triangle Shirtwaist Company,
    93
Trotsky, Leon, 130–131
Trotskyists, 130–131
Turbulent Thirties, 126–132
Twain, Mark, 46

unemployment, 14, 51, 126,
    129–130, 153
Union Pacific Railroad, 48
unions:
    Amalgamated Association of
        Iron, Steel and Tin
        Workers, 109
    Amalgamated Clothing
        Workers, 96, 124, 126–127
    Amalgamated Meat Cutters
        and Butcher Workmen,
        110
    American Federation of
        Labor, 70, 77, 78, 83, 89,
        93–95, 96, 99, 109,
        111–120, 127, 131–132,
        147

unions, *continued*
    American Federation of
        Labor and Congress of
        Industrial Organizations,
        30
    American Railway Union,
        68–69, 70–78
    Brotherhood of Locomotive
        Engineers, 51
    Brotherhood of Locomotive
        Firemen, 69
    Brotherhood of Railway
        Carmen, 112, 114
    as business, 80–81, 83
    business agents of, 84–88
    carpenters', 86
    Carriage and Wagon
        Workers' Union, 135–136
    Committee for Industrial
        Organization, 131–132
    company, 125–126
    Congress of Industrial
        Organizations, 83, 89, 131,
        133, 137–143, 147, *149*
    craft, 52, 69, 112, 131
    dues of, 15, 112
    Federal Society of
        Journeymen Cordwainers,
        16–20
    first, 14–15
    grocery workers', 89–91
    as illegal conspiracies,
        16–21, 37
    immigrants' fear of, 49
    industrial, 52, 96, 112, 131
    Industrial Workers of the
        World, 96–107, 110–111,
        132, 136, 137
    International Ladies'
        Garment Workers' Union,
        95–96, 126–127
    Knights of Labor, 35